Who Needs a World View?

Who Needs a World View?

Raymond Geuss

Harvard University Press

Cambridge, Massachusetts

London, England

2020

Second printing

Library of Congress Cataloging-in-Publication Data

Names: Geuss, Raymond, author.

Title: Who needs a world view? / Raymond Geuss.

Description: Cambridge, Massachusetts : Harvard University Press, 2020. |

Includes bibliographical references and index.

Identifiers: LCCN 2019054686 | ISBN 9780674245938 (cloth)

Subjects: LCSH: Perspective (Philosophy) | Belief and doubt.

Classification: LCC BD348 .G48 200 | DDC 140—dc23

LC record available at https://lccn.loc.gov/2019054686

Tabitha
ob. 08.XI.18
S.T.T.L.

Contents

À quoi sert d'agir, si la pensée qui guide l'action conduit à la découverte de l'absence de sens? Mais cette découverte n'est pas immédiatement accessible: il faut que je la pense, et je ne puis la penser d'un seul coup. Que les étapes soient douze comme dans le Boddhi; qu'elles soient plus nombreuses ou qu'elles le soient moins, elles existent toutes ensemble, et, pour parvenir jusqu'au terme, je suis perpétuellement appelé à vivre des situations dont chacune exige quelque chose de moi: je me dois aux hommes comme je me dois à la connaissance.

(Tristes Tropiques)

Preface

My most important teacher at university, Sidney Morgenbesser, used to play a game which I privately called "pantheons." (As far as I know, he himself had no word for the game.) As a good polytheist, Sidney thought that if there was such a thing as a god, there would *have to be* several such entities, and probably a whole hierarchy of beings of different ontological status, entertaining complicated relations with each other. If all the philosophers in history were considered to be the domain of reference, there would be the "major divinities," "minor deities," "demigods," "heroes," "mere humans," and "all-too-human humans" (a category, to be sure, which, for other reasons, held little interest for Sidney). Since Sidney was an extraordinarily gifted philosopher, he was more interested in the considerations one could marshal to place particular figures in a particular category—that is, in the question of what constituted being a "major divinity"—than he was in which particular person got placed in which box. So depending on the context and the way the discussion proceeded, different philosophers got shifted from one category to the other. One could also play the game with a restriction to a particular century, say 1850–1950 (a natural period to pick, if one were playing the game in, say, 1965). Despite the migration of philosophers from one group to another over time, there were some visible regularities, the most striking of which was Sidney's placement of Gödel toward the top, or even at the very top, of the celestial hierarchy. He said on several occasions that it might well turn out that Gödel was the most important philosopher of the century. (Did he mean 1850–1950, or was this, from the point of view of the late 1960s, a prediction about 1901–2001?) The reason for Gödel's preeminence, he said, was that "he helped us to think about how to structure our knowledge."

Kurt Gödel was born in 1906 in the small city of Brünn (Brno) in the Austro-Hungarian Empire—now in the Czech Republic—and died in Princeton, New Jersey, in 1978. In 1931 he published a short paper entitled "Über formal unentscheidbare Sätze der *Principia mathematica* und verwandter Systeme" ["On formally undecidable theorems of *Principia mathematica* and related systems"],[1] which made what might be thought to be a highly technical point about axiomatic systems. Simplifying enormously, the paper shows that, if one makes certain natural assumptions, it is impossible to get a closed, consistent, axiomatic system that will cover all of arithmetic. This turns out, as Sidney said, to have utterly devastating consequences for various traditional ways of thinking about the structure of our knowledge, modes of thought that have over the centuries percolated down to inform even our everyday ways of thinking. What could seem more natural to us than that our knowledge forms, or could be made to form, a system that was consistent and complete? Sidney himself drew from Gödel support for his particular version of Deweyite pragmatism: knowledge was best construed not as a closed axiomatised system of propositions, but as a series of repeated attempts by living agents to make the best of problematic situations, attempts that were at best more or less successful within some given context. What worked perfectly well in one context would not necessarily do so in some others. The idea—which the Deweyite attributed to holders of traditional conceptions of "truth," "knowledge," "evidence," and so forth—of something that was *completely* successful in *absolutely* all possible contexts was one that was not even false, because "all possible contexts" could not even be defined or made determinate, and hence made no sense. Consistency was important, only if it turned out to be important (which it sometimes was, but not always). Absolute "completeness" was a fantasy. Obviously, these are not the only possible conclusions that could be drawn from a study of Gödel, and any philosopher worth even a tiny pinch of salt will be able to give one an argument about at least one aspect or another of Sidney's views, provided that they could develop these views sufficiently fully to permit them to be discussed in a detailed way.

The chapters in this book are all, one might say, about ways of thinking about ethics, politics, and religion in the light of Gödel. Given that we are the limited and weak animals we are, and given that we live in a society, here in Europe at any rate, which has been subjected to over two thousand years of Platonic and Christian education, it seems to us perfectly natural to be concerned with the consistency of what we believe, and also with the consistency of the ways in which we act. It also seems natural for us to try to get a "*vue d'ensemble*," a global overview of, ideally, the *whole* of the universe and of the world which we inhabit. Similarly, what could be more unexceptional than to think that I have a life to live as an individual and that it is of great importance for me to get a "complete" global overview of that life as a whole, if only to try to make it (overall) "good" (in whatever sense of that term is applicable)?

We call global overviews of the world as a whole: world views, world pictures, or ideologies, or perhaps we speak of having a "metaphysics" or, indeed, a "philosophy." Political parties, religious groupings, occasionally even some aesthetic movements either coalesce around or secrete from within themselves platforms, manifestos, creeds, statements of principles and similar documents, the more ambitious of which might aspire to articulate in a consistent, exhaustive way a (or "the") global vision of the grouping in question. Much of traditional religiously based ethics is devoted to emphasising the importance of having the "right" views about the world as a whole: in the West this usually means the view that it is a unitary cosmos created and cared for in all its details by a benevolent god. As far as the human individual is concerned, both Plato (in *Republic*) and Christianity propagate the idea that each human must be ready to give an account of his or her whole life after death, in a context which gives this ability a special urgency because of the prospect of reward or punishment in an afterlife. This encourages us to try to think of our lives as a single whole even while we are living. In the modern world, other, more strictly economic forces exert pressure in the direction of thinking of each individual as having a single "life-plan," and considering the lack of such a plan as at least a potential defect.[2]

The chapters that form the bulk of this volume all try to get clearer about the role which such attempts to get a "full" and "complete" view of the world or of our own individual lives play in human society and in individual reflection and action, and about some of the difficulties which such attempts encounter. The reader will perhaps be struck by two further features of these chapters which may seem peculiar. The first is that they all exhibit very clearly my own reluctance to make an absolutely sharp distinction between (individual) ethics, politics, and religion, and also a perhaps equal disinclination to draw too sharp a boundary between purportedly general conceptual theoretical analysis and ratiocination, historical interpretation, and remembrance and reflection on individual experience, including aesthetic experience. It is right that I wish to blur these distinctions. Or rather that I don't think they were ever really very clear in the first place. In particular, I reject the idea that there is any such thing as a freestanding individual "ethics" prior to and independent of religion, sociology, economics, art / aesthetics, and politics. Certainly, there is nothing like a possible theoretical discipline of "individual ethics" that can be mastered and is not somehow dependent on *anything* else. This is one of the things which I think Hegel saw very clearly. In his philosophical work there is a detailed interlocking account of human social life, the economy, law, and politics—this is his *Rechtsphilosophie*—and there are separate accounts of art, religion, philosophy, and world history. He never wrote an "ethics." Of course,

there are parts of the *Rechtsphilosophie* that are more pertinent to individual choice and action than others are; but there are also parts of
other works of his that are equally relevant, and these parts can't be
neatly extracted and presented coherently by themselves—certainly
not in such a way as to constitute a "guide to individual life." As Hegel
himself says, if you want *that,* ask an experienced member of your
own particular society.[3] This does not imply that there are no individual ethical problems, or that there is nothing in general one can
say about human life (so that there are only descriptions of individual
events, decisions, actions, and sequences of consequences). It also does
not imply that there might not be better and less good ways of dealing
with some given problem, or that certain people might not be better
at giving advice than others are. Some people are generally more intelligent, better informed, more concerned than others—but those
who are good advisors are not "good" *by virtue of* mastery of a separate intellectual discipline called "ethics" which has strict boundaries
that can (and must) be policed.

There is certainly no science of "ethics." Plato was wrong: It is not
that our souls are really aboriginal unities, that we have somehow
fallen away from this primordial natural state or failed to understand
it, and that we need to get back to it. Since no such natural, given
unity exists, a fortiori we cannot use our "knowledge" of it to give
unity to our projects and thus be in a position to lead a good life.
Kant is right that whatever unity we *seem to* find in the world is unity
we actually *impose.* (He was merely wrong in thinking that the forms
of such imposition were significantly more fixed, universal, and invariable than they actually are.)

Whatever unity our drives, impulses, projects, beliefs, and commitments have is one that we have constructed. This construction
is one to which we have a strong tendency and perhaps a deep
commitment—a commitment so deep that it generates an illusion of
necessity and, perhaps, even of the ontological preexistence of what
it seeks—but to what extent it can succeed is always an open question, subject to the vagaries of the world and the accidents of history.

So the question should be *how* the construction should proceed, which constructions are possible and desirable, at what cost, and under what social and individual circumstances. Human life is the story of this recurrent need to orient ourselves toward some imagined unity, and the recurrent failure of our attempts to achieve it by construction. Seeing through this cycle no more prevents the illusion from recurring than eating breakfast prevents the recurrence of hunger in the evening.

The idealised bureaucrat who is Kant's model of the ethical subject[4] may imagine that subsumption under universal laws is the be-all and end-all of a good, valuable, attractive human life, but the observation that *anything* can be subsumed under a universal law (if one allows enough room for human ingenuity) means that this apparently strict requirement is actually empty. The real work in a Kantian scheme is done by the formulation of the individual maxim, but this is something Kant certainly does not encourage us to consider carefully—rather he strongly suggests that it is easy and unproblematic for us to know what maxim we are acting on. It is not, however, the case that we always clearly and transparently know on what maxim we are acting. It would, of course, make "ethics" very tidy if for any question we could respond (as utilitarians suggest) by saying *"calculemus,"*[5] but one would have to have a seriously deranged personality to consider tidiness the highest human virtue. If the attraction of both the Kantian and the utilitarian models depends to any significant extent on the power of the analogy with "real knowledge," as represented paradigmatically by mathematics, then Gödel's result should represent a significant shock to the system.

Individual "ethics" comes to be presented as a purportedly separate subject area and topic for a freestanding treatment under certain political and social circumstances; particularly when the world of politics seems to have moved completely out of the control of individuals—this is an archetypical Hegelian point (which he makes about the connection between the advent of the Roman Empire and the rise of stoicism).[6] So one can see it not as progress in the division of labour, but as an indirect indictment of a society that individual "ethics" comes in it to have special prominence as a purportedly separate discipline.

No amount of heroic courage, strength of will, or moral fibre is going to be able to compensate for having rotten social institutions. As Brecht once put it (in his *Galileo*): "Unhappy is the society that needs heroes."[7] It is perhaps "not my fault" if the institutions within which I find myself, and which I cannot change, do not permit *anyone* to lead a good or full life, but so what? Is my own personal purity always what is at issue? What does this very focus on what is or is not "the fault" of some individual tell us about the society in question? Or, for that matter, about an individual who is keen to make this claim? Is the attempt to avoid being at fault a good project for a whole human life? Is a society of people trying to develop and exercise their "moral fibre" actually all that attractive? To say grandly "dixi veritatem et salvavi animam meam" ["I've spoken the truth and saved my soul"][8] may be an impressive gesture, but why isn't a focus exclusively on the salvation of my soul also a sign of self-centredness? Maybe it is legitimate for *me* to be more concerned, within limits and in certain contexts, about *my own* intentions, motives, and actions than about yours, or his, or theirs, but this is certainly not obviously something for me to glory in. One might think that the historical movement in which theology and politics are gradually pushed aside by ethics and "culture" is simply part of a story of progressive rationalisation and human progress, but I am suggesting that the real story is much more complex than that, and that, although it is a story in which something is gained, it is also a tale of much that is lost.

The second feature of this volume which might seem surprising is the non-monographic approach—particularly, one might think, if I hold that there is something to regret in the isolation of "ethics" from theology, politics, art, and the study of history and society in general. Surely most of these subjects were in the past pursued not through aphorisms, individual essays on particular points, and brief critical interventions, but in a highly, one might say even excessively, systematic way. Aquinas's *Summa Theologica* or Hobbes's *Leviathan* or Marx's *Das Kapital* were the models—extensive, systematic works, not Montaigne, Friedrich Schlegel, Nietzsche, or Musil. So shouldn't a book that tries to ignore the boundaries between these disciplines be at least equally systematic? Of course, Gödel's results do not imply that it is impossible to summarise in an encyclopaedic way, at any given time, as many of the results of the pursuit of knowledge and of human reflection as possible. Rather, at best (or worst, depending on one's view) it implies that any such summary will not be at the same time absolutely consistent and absolutely complete.

Nietzsche, of course, raises another relevant question here. He is interested in another aspect of philosophy's obsession with systematicity. There is the issue of the sheer coherence of the idea that we could attain a single (axiomatised) system of all knowledge, and of the idea that our life as a whole could, or should, be seen through the lens of a technician who puts every decision of ours through a universalisation machine and files it according to the result. More importantly, though, traditional philosophers are motivated, Nietzsche believes, by commitment to a certain tacit moral ideal, one expressed perhaps most forcefully in ancient stoicism. This is the ideal of a human with an unchanging and invariable character, exhibiting great self-control and extreme fixity of purpose in the face of all the variable accidents of human life. The counterpart of this is the idea of a single, coherent, unchanging philosophical doctrine about the world as a whole and our place in it. This is turn means that the ideal form of philosophical writing should be the discursively monolinear monograph, developing a unitary world view, presenting arguments for it, refuting objections in a kind of timeless present (the illusion of which is easily attained in *written* texts). The sage has a unified personality *because* he subscribes to a unitary world view which he can express in a unitary monographic account of "the system of the world." Nietzsche thinks this complex has become problematic partly because we have come to see, more clearly than others before us did, the high cost imposed on self and others by the commitment to this ideal of the human personality.[9] Once we have seen through the sources of the obsession with unity, completeness, consistency, and invariability, we may become capable of seeing other possibly valuable ways of thinking and living. This collection of essays is informed, as mentioned above, by the general view that it is inadvisable to try to discuss and decide what is best to be done (including what it is best for an individual to do) while restricting oneself to the subject matter and method of the purported discipline of "ethics" and abstracting from what we know about society, history, politics, religion, and art. At the same time, it assumes that it is sometimes appropriate and useful to express thoughts about these subjects in the form of individual essays rather than of a unitary, systematic monograph.

Chapter 1 builds on ideas first discussed in "Pater Krigler," a piece Martin Bauer of the Hamburger Institut für Sozialforschung asked me to write as a brief "statement" about how I had originally become aware of Marxist theory and what I thought its continuing interest might be. This German language text was posted on *Soziopolis* on May 5, 2018. The text of Chapter 3 was first published in German as "Historisierung, Aufklärung, Genealogie," in *Filozofija I Društvo* 27, no. 1 (2016), pp. 189–202. The translation is my own. Chapter 5 was originally published as "The Metaphysical Need and the Utopian Impulse," in *Actions, Reasons and Reason*, edited by Ralf Stoecker and Marco Iorio (Berlin: De Gruyter, 2015). Chapter 6 was first published as "Manifestos and Confessions in the Art-World," *Cambridge Literary Review,* Issue 11: Manifestos, 2018. The text of Chapter 8 was originally published in German as "Metaphysik ohne Bodenständigkeit," in *Negativität,* edited by Thomas Khurana et al. (Berlin: Suhrkamp Verlag, 2018). The translation is my own. Every effort has been made to identify copyright holders and obtain permission for the use of copyrighted material. Notification of any additions of corrections that should be incorporated in future reprints or edition of this book would be greatly appreciated.

In writing these essays I have particularly profited from discussions of the topics treated here with Lorna Finlayson, Peter Garnsey, Gérald Garutti, Birte Löschenkohl, Brian O'Connor, Tim Mathews, Richard Raatzsch, and Tom Stern. Ian Malcolm has, as ever, been a model of editorial efficiency and judiciousness. I could not have written these essays without the support of Hilary Gaskin, to whom I owe by far my greatest debt of gratitude.

1

Who Needs a World View?

Et n'est train de vie si sot et si debile que celuy qui se conduict
par ordonnance et discipline.

(Montaigne)

"Proletarians of all countries, unite!" People who prick up their ears
and pay close attention to this, who begin to reflect on what it means
to them and how they should now think, feel, and behave, have a
world view. The same is true for those who have a similar reaction to
"Allons, enfants de la patrie" or to "O come, all ye faithful." A world
view is not in the first instance some kind of grand scientific theory
of the universe, but something that characteristically actively ad-
dresses particular people *by name*, telling them who they are and at
the same time imposing on them an identity. In the three cases I have
just cited, these identities are that of communist (seeing myself as proletarian, rather than, for instance, as merely a worker or as one of the
poor), of a patriotic French citizen (rather than just a peasant from
Poitou or a computer programmer from Lyon), or of a Christian (and
faithful member of the flock of Christ). As these cases indicate, there
are usually interconnected individual and collective aspects to this
identity: to be a proletarian is to see oneself as part of a group of a
certain kind. Following Althusser,[1] we might call this the "interpellative aspect" of a world view. I am addressed and stopped in my
tracks by the world view, encouraged to identify myself in the way it

suggests and accept the consequences.[2] Usually the identity one acquires by having a world view carries with it certain duties, expectations, or obligations. With the interpellation, there is often associated a historical or quasi-historical narrative and sometimes (although not always) a theory. The Christian has *Heilsgeschichte,* the nationalist the story of the formation, the trials, the successes, and the failures of the nation, the Communist the story of original accumulation, the transition from slave societies to feudalism to capitalism, with the prospect of a classless society in the future. This narrative gives special density, meaning, and concreteness to the identity the world view inculcates.[3] Do we all have world views? Do we need them?

Béla

In the autumn of 1959, I was twelve years old and starting as a boarder in a Hungarian Catholic school not far from Philadelphia, Pennsylvania. The school had been set up and was run by and for refugees after the failed uprising in 1956 (together with a sprinkling of priests from the Spanish provinces of the same religious order and a handful of boys from Latin America). I was one of the two or three boys there in response to a public announcement in one of the regional Catholic newspapers of bursaries available to potential pupils who scored sufficiently well on the entrance examination. I listened attentively to Father Krigler (Béla) who was to teach us "Religion." He began by explaining that there were really only two major spiritual powers in the world, two coherent and complete world views: Catholicism and Communism.[4] Krigler was a Catholic priest who had been born in 1925 in the small town of Csongrad and had lived through the late 1940s in Hungary. He was anything but a Communist himself; however, he was also no fool, and he was morally fastidious enough to disdain to jump on the fashionable anti-Communist bandwagon,[5] and take cheap shots at something which one made no attempt to understand. He repeated again and again that although some views were too frivolous or implausible even to take seriously, Communism did not fall into that category and was something one needed to understand as fully and correctly as possible, even if, as he thought one must, one had to reject it. In addition, he added, fairness required one to admit that, at that moment—unfortunately, in his view—Communism had an enormous cognitive and philosophical advantage over Catholicism. The Communist world view rested on the philosophy of Hegel, as interpreted, filtered, modified, and adapted by Marx, and was making some attempt to take account of the modern world. Catholicism, in contrast, had taken fright at the pace of social change in the late nineteenth century and tried to withdraw into itself altogether by nailing its colours to a particularly sclerotic form of late Aristotelianism, the philosophy of Thomas Aquinas. Aristotle, and also Thomas, were important systematic philosophers who had some significant strengths, but they also had one particular, and fatal, weakness. There was an Aristotelian, and thus also a Thomist, concept of "development" in the sense of biological growth—a tree grew out of an acorn, a human being was generated by two other human beings—but, history, real human history, was something radically different from the "genesis, growth, and development" which one found in the natural world. Aristotle and Thomas simply provided no conceptual tools for the theoretical understanding of history. Book I of the *Metaphysics* is not a counter-instance to this but a model of how *not* to do history (in this specific case the history of philosophy). Aristotle knows that his own doctrine is the true, "perfect (*teleion*) form" of philosophy, just as the fully developed tree is the perfect form which the acorn "is potentially" and is striving or aspiring to become, and in his "history" of the subject, he shows how previous philosophers are his precursors, their doctrines "leading up to" the truth his views instantiate.[6] Nature is an unendingly recurring cycle: acorns grow into trees that produce acorns. Human history, as far as it is visible to Aristotle at all, is about similar natural developments and recurrent cycles. What is important about an acorn is that, unless circumstances are too unpropitious, it will "naturally" develop into the perfection of a tree, when the cycle will begin again. Similarly, humans are "naturally" beings who are "political"; that is, they live in city-states (*poleis*), if conditions are sufficiently propitious for city-states to be established. The only philosophically relevant thing to say about historical change in city-states is that there are a small number of ways in which they may be constituted (monarchy, oligarchy, democracy, and perhaps some variants on these). There will be sequences of orderly transformations of one of these constitutions into another: monarchies will be replaced by oligarchies, which in turn will give way to democracies, which in turn will break down into chaos resulting in the reestablishment of some kind of one-man rule. There will be a cycle here, as there is a cycle in the transformation of acorns into trees into acorns. That is all one can say philosophically about history.

There were, potentially, other models around for Aristotle to have tried to adapt and develop, but neither Herodotus nor Thucydides seem to have been of the least interest to him.[7] A further possibility would have been Aeschylus's *The Oresteia,* which begins in a world much like that envisaged by Aristotle: an unending cycle of murders, each breeding a desire for revenge and thus generating more murders and more desire for vengeance. However, the third play (*The Eumenides*), dramatises how things can change. In this play the cycle is broken and something *new* emerges—a court, which, by taking punishment out of the hands of individual relatives or clans, lays the basis for a very different kind of human association: the democracy. To be sure, in Aeschylus, the court is founded (and thus legitimised) by a superlatively intelligent and skilled "goddess" (Athena), who thinks it out in advance and imposes it in a single act. This is still a mythical account, but it could have been the beginning of something more. To get "real" history, one would have to de-theologise the story, disposing of the gods and goddesses and focusing on human action (in its natural and social environment). One would have had to recognise that there probably was no *single* act of "founding the democracy," but a series of differing projects and actions by a number of different people and groups over time. Finally, one would have had to realise that many, if not all, of the individuals and groups involved were not, at the start, at all clear about what they were doing and would have been completely surprised by the outcome: whatever Kleisthenes intended or did in his reforms,[8] he didn't in any interesting sense "intend to establish the democracy"; it is only in retrospect that we can see that what he did contributed to that result.

Even if Thomas Aquinas did not read Greek and could have had no access to a manuscript of *The Oresteia,* he could still, in principle, instead of simply following Aristotle into the darkness, have found traces of a different and non-Aristotelian, Christian view, which had a place for history, in Augustine. Augustine did see that human history was not merely a cycle of recurrent developing (or even developing and degenerating) natural forms. The form of life in the Garden of Eden ended for good with Adam's Fall, a human act which changed everything, just as the Incarnation, a divine initiative, again changed everything. Aquinas, however, did his best to ignore this or to force it into completely inappropriate Greek ontological categories.[9]

Hegel, in fact, was the first philosopher who fully understood that history needed to be brought into philosophy and philosophy into history. To understand the human world, you have to understand its history, and that means always being able to adopt two different points of view on past events at the same time: first, the retrospective glance of the philosopher who knows ex post facto where everything is in fact going to end up (because, in fact, it has already ended up there), *but then also* the views of the historical participants, who are ignorant of the future and precisely do *not* know what will really eventually happen. The "Introduction" to Hegel's *Phänomenologie* shows clearly that Hegel sees the integration of these two perspectives as the key to understanding the human world. The cognitive superiority of Communism consisted precisely in the fact that its founder, Marx, had really understood and made this basic insight fully his own.[10]

Over the weeks and months of the course, Father Krigler continued: The sorts of cognitive options and positions that were on offer to us in the public sphere (that is, those that were on offer on the East Coast of the United States in 1959, three years after the uprising in Hungary),[11] were all just variants of "liberalism," which was a clumsy and completely unphilosophical rubbish heap of narrow-minded prejudices, bits of wishful thinking, and random observations. Liberalism was just a particularly debased and etiolated form of ancient humanism. Whatever its historical importance, humanism in the modern world faced the insuperable objection that it was unable to give an answer to the question why it was a good idea to do the "human(e) thing." This certainly was not obviously a worthy moral ideal, if it meant developing and exercising those capacities that were specific to humans, as opposed to animals. As he pithily and tartly put it, this would mean that killing millions of Jews for imaginary reasons would be particularly praiseworthy because no animal would do something like that.[12] This was parallel to the arguments against the Thomist obsession with "human nature" and "natural law." An ethics could not be founded on *any* such notions because, as he put it, even if one granted (which he didn't) that it made sense to think about ethics in terms of a "human nature," the most important thing about that *human* nature would have to be that humans could act *against* "nature."

Like Thomism, modern liberalism had no useful concept of history,[13] and was thus completely incapable of allowing one to understand anything much about human societies, the way they really operated, and the way they changed. In addition to this, though, liberalism had two further insuperable problems. First, although it might occasionally present itself as a way of resolving conflict, it actually presupposed that society was essentially already at peace; that is, it had attained a state in which all the real vital questions of life were either settled or could be put aside for later (for a "later" that perhaps would never come). In addition, liberalism started from a particularly silly and unreflective form of individualism. It was important, Father Krigler went on, not to misunderstand this. Neither Catholicism nor Communism were actually anti-individualist. Rather, both thought that the "individual" (differently understood by each of these two movements, of course) was an important goal or *telos,* but also one that could only be attained through a complicated series of historical, social, and political developments and forms of training. What was wrong with liberalism was that it characteristically started from the idea of an abstract, naked "individual" who was somehow an ontological and psychological "given," waiting out there as a normal part of the furniture of the world, and whose unfiltered and uncorrected beliefs and desires could be a source of legitimacy for action.

Both Catholicism and Communism (explicitly in Lenin and Trotsky)[14] agreed that there were certain crude rules of thumb that, more or less, were accepted in most human societies: don't steal, don't kill innocent people, don't use insulting language to your neighbours. They weren't anything like strict rules because they were too "empty," too vaguely formulated, and admitted of too many exceptions; they were also not universally accepted in absolutely all societies, but they were rough and ready expressions of some basic ways of facilitating human interaction and reducing conflict. One such principle was that, other things being equal, it was probably a good idea not to interfere with what people thought and did, unless it impinged in an immediate and vivid way on other people. One should depart from this rule only if one had a very good reason. The valuelessness of this as anything like a strict rule was indicated by the fact that "other things" were in fact *never* equal, what counted as a "good reason" was almost always up for grabs, and what was "vivid and immediate" for one person need not be so for others. The emptiness of most of these rules of thumb was masked to most people in most societies most of the time, because of the social consensus that existed about *which* dimensions were the "obviously relevant" ones along which to measure whether "other things" were "equal" and what counted as a "good reason."

Not all social conflict was in all circumstances a bad thing: societies in which subjugated groups were making a fuss and trying to
threaten the social consensus might well be thought to be in a better
state than those in which the oppressed were silent and passive. Still,
in any given society, if one did not wish specifically to rock the boat
of existing social consensus, one might think that these moral rules
of thumb (such as they were) gave you some kind of general orientation. The same might be true of the principle of not interfering with
others (without a good reason). What this rule very definitely did *not*
do, however, was give you any reason to believe that the desires,
wishes, and preferences people happened to think they had, had any
special or foundational status for social ethics. It was not true that
people even in most cases were the best judges of what they thought.
On most subjects they wouldn't antecedently have a view at all, but
would be tempted to make one up, *if asked.* It wasn't true that people
were themselves the best judges of what they wanted or desired. Krigler was a keen student of psychoanalysis and thought that it had once
and for all put paid to any assumption of that kind. Finally, it was
obvious, and had been so since the time of Plato, that people were
not spontaneously the best judges of what was in their own interest.
None of these questions—What do I think? What do I want? What
is in my interest?—could be answered either by simply asking the
person involved to express his or her opinion, or by simple empirical
observation of their actions. Answering any of them required a tre-
mendously complex and effortful, theoretically informed enquiry.
The situation was even worse if one changed the question to (for instance) what is in *"our"* interests, which by no stretch of the imagination could be discovered by simple summation of suffrages.

Rather than taking expressed beliefs and desires at face value, both
Catholicism and Communism, in contrast to liberalism, looked very
seriously at the context within which beliefs and desires were formed
and the possible distortions that could be and were imposed by factors
beyond the control of the individuals in question. Catholicism
thought the human will (and consequently also human cognition)

was inherently corrupted by original sin, and Communists had complex views about the ideological distortion of belief and the mechanisms for the deformation of human desire in capitalist societies. Both recognised that this meant that one must treat actual expressions of belief and desire as material to be understood and analysed, rather than as the final word on anything in particular.

Knowing one's own mind was not the natural state of most adults most of the time, but rather it was either a signal achievement of a few resulting from a combination of extreme good luck and enormous moral and intellectual effort (Plato), or it was an unending process that could never be completed (Augustine), or it might turn out that there was no "mind" there to know and that the illusion of unitariness dissolved under close inspection (Lacan?), or that *really* knowing one's own mind was fatal (early Nietzsche)—especially in an era in which large private corporations with vested economic interests could wield such huge power to "form opinion" and shape or even generate desire.[15] To act as if people whom we know to be confused, uncertain, deceived, often abused, and distracted, were the automatic and absolute sovereign experts both on their own desires and the social good, was manifest folly. It was not to "treat them as adults" or "treat them with the respect they deserved," and it certainly did not do them any kind of favour. Rather it was a recipe for cultural degeneration, moral confusion, and political and social regression. There were, of course, certain things you were not allowed to do to them, although they were deceived, but that was a separate issue.

Slavery was a terrible individual misfortune in the ancient world and a deep and unforgivable social evil in the modern world, but "freedom" alone, although it might be the dearest aspiration of a slave, did not actually tell one anything much about what might be a valuable way to spend one's life as a free person.[16] Liberalism's much vaunted "freedom" did not amount, as one could see by simply looking around, to much more than the unlimited consumer choice of the members of a population who were allowed to remain uninformed, undisciplined, and mentally and emotionally stunted, or, even worse, were intentionally kept in this state, manipulated, deceived, and actively mystified. The political freedom on offer was equally not much more than, at most, the ability to pick almost at random between two forgettable candidates from two virtually indistinguishable parties.[17] It was wrong, a sin, and deeply shameful to oppress, abuse, take advantage of, or even hold in contempt those who through no fault of their own had not been able to develop certain capacities of discrimination and ratiocination, or whose taste was uncultivated, but it was a very long step from that to declaring the absolute sovereignty of "individuals" even in their most uninformed, undisciplined, and undeveloped state. "Condescension" was partly a matter of manner and style, but there was nothing inherently condescending about refusing to take all opinions, tastes, and preferences to be equally good.

The consumer world, full of an infinite quantity and variety of commodities all being loudly promoted, is something that we take for granted.[18] If we don't, we at least are encouraged to assume that those who do not have access to this world would like nothing more than to enter it as fully fledged, fully engaged (and monetarily adequately endowed) members. It was a very important experience for me to see, at a young and impressionable age, that this is not the only possible reaction one could have. It would be hard to overestimate the shock, confusion, and trauma which Hungarian emigrants in the late 1950s experienced when they first encountered this huge, creepy, unknown universe with its mysterious laws and puzzling customs. Several of them said to me more or less the same thing: They could understand why there might be two kinds of soap in the shops—a strong kind for deep, persistent stains and a milder kind for the face; maybe there might be a reason to have three or four different kinds, although it wasn't clear what that reason would be, but there couldn't possibly be any reason for there to be twenty different kinds of soap. There must be something wrong there. Either there really was no difference between most of them, and then the potential buyer was being imposed on, deceived, and duped: he was enticed into spending his time trying to figure out what non-existent differences there were between them. (The parallel to the political situation was obvious.) Or there were some arcane differences between them, but who was such a shallow person that he had nothing better to do with his time than try to distinguish between types of soap? Our economic system predisposes us to think that "choice" (especially consumer choice) is exceedingly important and that the larger the range of products on offer the greater our freedom. But, as Krigler would have put it, the notion of variety of consumer choice is dialectical: at a certain point more reverses itself into less. Your power of effective choice between three kinds of soap (mild, strong, and very expensive and pampering) may be greater by virtue of being limited than is a choice between thirty soaps, because then the choice set becomes unsurveyable except by virtue of exerting oneself to an extent not warranted by the value of the choice. Making simple consumer choices was not actually that important and should not be made that difficult.

Sartre may have thought that we were all forced to be free; this was perhaps unfortunate, but we should embrace it. Hungarians arriving in the United States often had the sense that their lives were being coarsened by being *forced* into situations of choice they would have preferred to avoid, and they resented this. If you asked for soap in the shop, no one would give you soap;, instead you got an interminable song-and-dance about brands, at the end of which you were none the wiser and you then had to "make a decision." Why would you want to do that? It was just soap. And once you had "chosen" a soap, you had to move on to the same degrading torment about toothpaste, loo roll, and shoe polish. The worst part of it was that this was presented as being in your own interest, whereas it was clearly in the interest of those who produced and sold soap. This was to add insult to injury. "Choice" in general was overrated. One also did not "choose" a religion or "choose a world view" as if they were different types of soap. Of course, there was a voluntative element involved, but it looked nothing like "consumer choice." If you didn't like a soap, you could put it away and never use it; however, to "choose" a world view was to commit oneself to it, and once you committed yourself, you were a changed person. So at both ends of the spectrum, the trivial and the anything-but-trivial, "choice" was not the be-all and end-all of human life.[19]

So why did liberalism (in one form or another) seem to be the only game in (our) town? The United States was, Krigler said, particularly favoured by history and geography. It had been able to exterminate the natives, and it had no enemies on its immediate borders: Canada and Mexico were not threats. Liberalism could thus maintain itself in the United States for as long as its bounty of unexhausted natural resources lasted, and its military power and industrial strength were undiminished. And for as long as that was the case, the United States could stave off internal threats from its own population with promises of increasing material prosperity, and it could afford to ignore the problems of the rest of the world. To be sure, Africa, Latin America, and Asia would very soon become independent agents and players in world politics, and not just geographic regions that could be treated as areas for colonial domination. As soon as that happened, a new world system would evolve, and then, at the latest, it would become clear that liberalism had nothing to offer. The true face of US-style "liberalism," hiding its true nature, as was to be expected, behind a mask which represented it as being the very opposite of what it really was, would only emerge sixty years later with the election of Donald Trump.

Krigler thought that it was in general always a good idea to look at the reverse, the inverse, or the exact opposite of what people said. This was particularly true in politics. Assertions did not come from nowhere; they were generally motivated. Where was the lack or deficiency or negation—the empty space—that motivated the assertion? Sometimes what one found was an aspiration. There was a recognition that something was lacking and the assertion was an attempt to motivate people to remedy that: it was a country that, despite its many good qualities, was not particularly well-ordered or progressive (Brazil) that inscribed the words "Ordem e Progresso" on its national

flag. However, sometimes what was revealed was something much
more interesting. Speech was an attempt actively to maintain the deficient state in existence, generate well-focused ignorance or divert
attention away from some empty space—for instance, when British
commentators in the eighteenth century pointed out that it was
Virginia slaveholders who shouted loudest about "liberty," or, to take
an example from a later period, when the US commander in occupied Iraq warned the Iranians not to be tempted to intervene in the
internal affairs of a sovereign foreign state.

I have mentioned a number of respects in which Father Krigler's
observations seem to have been particularly astute and remarkably
prescient, so, lest it be supposed that my attitude toward him has remained uncritical or even hagiographic, let me mention a few of his
opinions that have not, in my view, stood the test of time so well.
Although he was perfectly right that world hegemony of Europe and
North America was already visibly nearing its end, his vision of the
future was very much focused specifically on Africa, where he seemed
to expect that a number of new nations, eager for responsibility and
brimming over with energy, would establish themselves as major economic, scientific, political, and cultural powers. I am afraid I think
he was influenced here by wishful thinking. He at one point suggested to me that I try to study Swahili, if I had a chance, at university; I think he believed that it might establish itself as a kind of pan-
African lingua franca. Krigler also had an odd, slightly Viennese
obsession with statistics, inductive logic, and probability theory. He
insisted that I make sure to acquire training in these areas at university because it would be very useful whatever else I decided to do. I
suspect this was because he was overly impressed that even the basic
laws of nature might not conform to certain naive notions of certainty
and determinateness. I did follow this bit of advice until it became
clear to me that, although statistics was a perfectly respectable technical discipline with many uses, I was not able to see the purportedly more universal implications of this body of material that he
seemed to have thought it had. I have sometimes wondered how my

life would have been different if I had become, for instance, a Swahili-speaking statistician at a Catholic establishment in East Africa instead of a Cambridge philosopher.

I did not find myself able to respond to Father Krigler's eloquent appeals to help free Catholicism from the "sarcophagus of Thomism" (as he called it) and to adapt it to the new world society that was arising. This project didn't seem to me likely to be achievable, and would in any case, as I increasingly came to think, be of at best questionable desirability. It certainly had no attraction for me. Nevertheless, even sixty years later, his acuity of perception, his prescience, and his judgment amaze me, and, his basic analysis, subject only to a very few minor revisions, still seems to me convincing. Certainly it was deeply influential on me and structured my thinking, although, at about the same time as I left for university in New York in 1963, he moved to what was for me the Far West (Buffalo, New York), and I never saw him again. I did, however, have one déjà-vu experience concerning him. During my first term at university, I read Thomas Mann's *Der Zauberberg* and had the uncanny sense that Mann had known Krigler and modeled Naphtha, the Jewish orphan boy who becomes an ultra-leftist Jesuit and radical scourge of all forms of "humanism," on him. Actually, we know that Naphtha was modelled on a Georg Lukács, a completely different Hungarian (and one-time Commissar in the Budapest Soviet Republic after World War I), who was of Mann's own generation.[20]

Sidney

The intellectual father-figure space did not, however, remain unoccupied for long, because in my second year I encountered Sidney Morgenbesser. Sidney was a great admirer of the pragmatism of John Dewey, and he began his course "Introduction to Philosophy," as he often did, with a discussion of Dewey's "Reconstruction in Philosophy."[21] Philosophy, he said, arose when human social interaction was disrupted or rendered uncomfortable because traditional beliefs and values were disturbed, especially by new forms of knowledge: when traditional Greek beliefs and values were felt to be under attack by the new skills and sciences—"rhetoric," "logic (of a kind)," and so forth—professed and propounded by the sophists, or traditional Christianity was thought to be undermined by Newtonian science. Philosophy was a way of trying to restore smooth functioning, and the question it asked was what had to change for smooth and harmonious interaction to be reestablished? In the past, philosophy had generally been conservative, inventing ways to preserve existing values unchanged or, at any rate, to replace them with only minimally modified versions of themselves. It did this by insulating them from subversion by the new techniques and forms of knowledge. Thus, Plato's metaphysics was developed in order to ground and reinstate the (slightly, but really only very slightly, modified) versions of the generally accepted Greek virtues of manliness, justice, moderation, and the rest by rooting them in a purported form of knowledge ("dialectic") that made them impervious to sophistic arguments. Kant's metaphysics (and his epistemology) played a parallel role in defending (modified versions of) Christian freedom and responsibility against what was taken to be the universal causal determinism of physics. Philosophy should, however, give up this role of conservative watchdog and automatic defender of past values, and devote itself to a more flexible and forward-looking engagement with all forms of enquiry that would allow us to "reconstruct" our given values intelligently in the light of the current and emerging forms of knowledge. This seemed perfectly correct as an analysis of the past, but it did not really make it very clear how one was now to proceed. We should not simply cling to our old values mindlessly, but this does not really in itself tell us how we should "reconstruct" them. Sidney used to say that pragmatism was certainly true; the only problem was that it didn't work. Apart from being a clever, dialectical joke of the kind he specialised in, or rather of one of the kinds he specialised in, this has always struck me as a very profound statement, if one that it is rather difficult to get to the bottom of.

The best way to understand the pragmatists was by contrasting their position with a traditional and widely held view of human knowledge, its nature, and the role it could and did play in human life, which they were keen to reject. This traditional view had been gradually elaborated for over two thousand years and had gradually trickled down into everyday language and established itself as part of "common sense," so much so, in fact, that it was difficult for those of us who stood at the end of this long development to see it as a "theory" at all, rather than as simply a statement of something self-evident. It was, however, anything but self-evident, and it was important, for various reasons which the pragmatists thought they could specify, to see how this traditional view led us astray. Given its long history, it would be no surprise that it existed in an almost unsurveyable multitude of different variants. This made it especially difficult to criticise because like much of "common sense" it constituted a vague and also perpetually moving target. Still, all the variants of the traditional view had in common a kind of obsession with "truth." This "truth" was categorically singular and had a kind of absolute and timeless standing; if it was "true" that water was H_2O, then that was true at all times and places and in all contexts (and no alternative to this statement, such as that water was H_3O, was also true). When humans tried to orient themselves, they characteristically, and "naturally," tried to discover "the truth" about the situation in which they found themselves. The human ideal was to have "the" full truth about the world, that is, a complete and perfect image, or mirror, or picture or representation of the world as it really is—or at least, if one had reservations about the use of terms like "picture" or "image," a true statement that corresponded (or "was adequate") to the way the world is. It is this last part (truth as image or correspondence) which is absolutely indispensable to the traditional view, but which shows in a particularly visible way some of the difficulties associated with this position. They are multitudinous and have been extensively canvassed. For the view to make sense, it would seem to presuppose that one could give some content to the idea that there are two different, fully distinct things. There would have to be, on the one hand, the world as a bare reality, existing in itself, and independent of our ways of conceptualising it or of formulating anything about it in a set of propositions. Then, on the other hand, there were our concepts, propositions, and theories. It was hard to believe that the former, the bare world in itself, could be said to exist at all. If it did, by hypothesis we wouldn't be able to conceptualise it or say anything about it. Furthermore, what did, and could, "correspondence" mean between two things like the world and a set of propositions, two things that were so fundamentally different in nature? Two triangles could have "corresponding angles" but how could a banana "correspond" to a string quartet? "Truth is 'correspondence to / with the world'" might seem like a joke in any case because it simply replaced one term about which question had been raised ("truth") with another that was even more dubious.

The central idea of pragmatism was to reject most of this traditional image. People were not inherently entities who set out to map, reflect, mirror, or find beliefs that "corresponded" to the way the world really was in itself; rather they were highly developed animals, capable of various forms of action, speech, and mentation, who sometimes found themselves in "problematic situations" which they needed to deal with. Such situations arise when my smooth, routinised interactions with the world are interrupted in some way, so that I cannot proceed; as we might say, "I don't know how to go on." In such a situation I am looking not for an idea or theory that correctly mirrors the world, the "truth," but for something that "works," that gets rid of the obstacle I have encountered and allows me to go ahead with what I am trying to do. If I want to get honey from a beehive that is out of my reach, I don't want a theory of the honeybee; I want a stick to knock the hive down, or a ladder to put against the tree as a rudimentary aid to climbing it. Similarly, as Marx puts it, if I am drowning, I don't want a book on how to swim; I want to have acquired the muscle strength and coordination and the practical skill which will allow me to float or swim (or, we can add, I want an actual, physical life preserver). The solution to my problem will be not a time-less proposition, but something deeply dependent on what I am trying to do at the moment, what other powers and resources I have, and innumerable other aspects of the concrete situation. Eventually, with luck, I and my society may develop beyond made-up individual jerry-rigging in the use of individual tools, and we may move on to such things as sophisticated systematic usage of one of our most important tools, language, and to science, which involves intentional manipulation of the environment (experiment) and the use of statements in language or mathematical formulae. We develop complex standards of acceptability for these statements, which standards themselves gradually change over time. They are nothing but gener-alised canons of the kind of thing that we have found in the past will "work," that is will put an end to problematic situations we encounter and allow us to continue to do what we wish to do in a smooth and unimpeded way. Methods of enquiry and standards of acceptability are, of course, themselves evolving historically in tandem with our ability to deal with the world, and our "knowledge" of it. "Scientific method" itself is not a kind of timeless Platonic ideal with universal application everywhere and in all contexts, but a developing body of practices and techniques that have shown themselves to be helpful in solving the problems we have faced. There will, of course, at any given time and in any given place be accepted standards of what can and what cannot be asserted with any kind of warrant, a kind of "state of the art" of the methods of enquiry, but it will be historically vari-able and contextually polymorphous. In principle one could imagi-natively construct or create some standards of acceptability (of "war-ranted assertability," as pragmatists who follow Dewey sometimes call them) that are more strict than those we at the moment happen to impose, but this is a proleptic exercise of the imagination and it is of strictly limited value. *Some* minimal prevision is unavoidable and as such perfectly justifiable, but beyond our very restricted range of vi-sion, the future can be expected to hold surprises for us. Just as Marx-ists claim that large-scale "utopian speculation" about the future is empty and futile, either wishful thinking, an exaggerated projection of current fears, or just an extrapolation of present trends, pragmatists insist that the future is open, and we don't know which features of our present situation are fads, idiosyncratic accidents, or passing phases, and which are not. If we did know this, we would not be in the situation in which we find ourselves. The concept of "truth" as traditionally understood prevents us from focusing appropriately on this openness and changeability of human experience, and thus constitutes an obstacle to free enquiry and human growth.

If the pragmatist is called on to give an account of the old traditional view he or she is trying to undermine and reject, he or she might say something like the following: first of all, one should not assume that speaking of "truth" (the noun) is all that usual or is part of our everyday discourse. We generally do not say "It is true that it is raining," when we can say "It is raining." "True / truth" are generally used in everyday life not to change or modify what we say, but to give it more weight or emphasis. That is, their use is hortatory or argumentative. "It is true that it is raining" doesn't *mean* anything more than "It is raining"; it has, some would say, the same cognitive content (although perhaps a different rhetorical force). So if I say that Tabitha is in the garden, and, when someone who is sitting down and cannot see so clearly what I see, questions what I see with my own eyes, I can respond by saying "It is *true* that Tabitha is now in the garden." To say this is not to add something to the observation that Tabitha is in the garden, it is just to put it in a way that makes clear that I am aware of what he said and that I reject it. Of course, there is nothing whatever illicit or illegitimate about the use of rhetorical techniques to call people's attention to things they might otherwise overlook, or to emphasise that one is disagreeing with what someone else has said. However, it would be a mistake to reify what is merely a functional property of certain ways of speaking emphatically into a full-blown separate *property:* (the) Truth.

When traditionalists speak of some individual statement being "true" in some particular context, such as that it is true that it is now raining, or that it is true that Tabitha is now in the garden, although speaking in that way is unusual (except in highly particular contexts), what they say makes perfect sense. It means if we were to use the best methods available to us—in this particular case, simple observation would usually suffice—one would see that it was raining or Tabitha was in the garden, and if we wanted to go beyond that, we might say that, given our best methods, it was *warranted for* anyone to assert that it was raining or Tabitha was in the garden. "Truth," is, from another point of view, a completely dispensable notion; if one wishes to use the term at all, it means "warranted assertability," but why persist in using it, when one had seen it for what it was, a simple rhetorical grace note? So the traditional view was not "false," but just pointless (at best) and potentially misleading, given that it predisposed one to think of enquiry not as a series of open-ended projects, but as fixedly terminating in a reliably and invariant state of "true knowledge." The idea of Truth didn't work; it was a "one-size-fits-all" response to constantly changing problematic situations, a hindrance to, rather than a facilitator of, successful enquiry and human well-being.

Closely associated with, although not exactly the same as, this doctrine of "truth," its meaning and role in human life, was the view that we must have a world view, a final, true, certain theory which gives us full orientation in life. Sidney thought that Gödel and Tarski had certainly seriously dented the plausibility of this, and perhaps even irremediably destroyed it.[22] They certainly gave support to a basically pragmatist way of looking at the world. If, as Gödel had shown, you couldn't even get a complete and consistent formal theory of elementary mathematics, what chance did you have of getting a consistent and complete theory of "everything?" Tarski's "semantic theory of truth" was also taken to be correctly understood as deflationary.

Dewey's diagnosis and criticism of the conservative bias of the grand tradition of philosophy in *Reconstruction in Philosophy* seemed exceedingly persuasive, but the "positive recommendation" one could extract from it—namely: "Change your values and beliefs so as to make them compatible with news skills, techniques and forms of knowledge, but *without* simply trying to reinstate the old values 'unreconstructedly'"—did not really seem to be adequately informative. What exactly did it mean? What precise direction did it give? Having, since my first encounter with Dewey in 1964, read Adorno, I am inclined to think that what I took to be a deficiency could in fact be seen as a great contribution to understanding something very important, although I am not sufficiently knowledgeable about Dewey's views to know whether or not this could have been part of his intention. The absence of an algorithm or recipe for appropriate "progressive" reconstruction draws attention to the fact that we expected such a recipe and are bitterly disappointed at not finding one. Perhaps that expectation is precisely the problem, what we need to disabuse ourselves of. Why should there be anything like an antecedently fixed way of responding, and even if there were to be, why expect "philosophers" (that is people trained in the mode of thinking inculcated by Plato, Aristotle, Descartes, Kant, and Frege) to be able to provide them? Isn't the point of pragmatism that the "new" and the unexpected really do exist? Situations change and new problems emerge, requiring new solutions. Why assume that study of "old" problems, or the specific ways in which people went about dealing with the old problems, will give you an inside track on dealing with the new? Especially if, as a good pragmatist, you think that previous "solutions" have not been closer and closer approximations to access the eternal truth, but simply tricks, gadgets, instruments, and such that happened to work?

At first glance, pragmatism would seem to be very bad news for Father Krigler, undercutting and rendering irrelevant his whole mode of argumentation. After all, his (tacit, but firm) assumption was that humans must have a world view, a universal form of orientation in the world, and the only question was which one. One way of taking pragmatism is as denying that assumption. Krigler, of course, was quite familiar with claims of this general kind. Heidegger's *Holzwege*

contained a famous essay, "Die Zeit des Weltbildes,"[23] which put the
point very clearly and persistently that the very idea of (having a)
world view is not a timeless given, but something that arose only gradually over the course of time and makes sense only during a limited
(if perhaps, by the standards of an individual human life, long) historical epoch. In particular, it presupposes a whole complicated metaphysical apparatus: the conception of "substance," a distinction between subject and object, a highly developed, but, Heidegger thinks,
dubious and distorting theory of human subjectivity and its modes
of access to the world, theories of appearance, of the image, of representation, and perhaps "correspondence." None of these conceptions
existed from time immemorial—rather they were specific creations
at particular times. The very fact that the world presented itself as
something which could be "pictured" was a distortion, although how
we could now rid ourselves of it was anything but clear.

Krigler might have responded that pragmatism itself was clearly a
world view, perhaps despite its protestations of not being one, but this
"*tu quoque*" retort is so predictable and lame as to be unworthy of
consideration. In any case, it would just seem to show that the notion of "world view" itself is contested and not very clear, and the
more that is the case, the more useless one might think it becomes
for marking any serious distinction, and the whole discussion
threatens to become pointless. If that were to be the case, the pragmatist would have won by default.

Krigler did think he had a response of a different kind. Neither
Catholicism nor Communism pretend they are timeless—rather, they
explicitly locate themselves in history, that is, in a particular human
history. This is slightly obscure in the case of Catholicism because of
the practical necessities of everyday preaching in a society such as ours
and also the deleterious anti-historicist influence of Thomas Aquinas,
but it is still very clearly visible in some pre-Thomist versions, for instance (as Krigler was keen to point out), Augustine. There was no
Catholicism—no complex system of sacraments, no dogmas, no
clergy, and no Pope—in the garden of Eden, or before Christ's res-

urrection, and there would be none again at the end of time, when the divine presence would be immediate (or, perhaps, immediate for some and completely absent for others). Equally, Krigler insisted, Communists, at least the reflective and theoretically sophisticated among them, realised that their world view was a function of the transition period between the Industrial Revolution and the advent of the classless society and that there was nothing wrong with it for all that (that is because it did not instantiate some purported "eternal Truth"). Marx was clear enough that "communisms" before industrialisation were nothing but utopian illusions, if illusions that, for perfectly comprehensible reasons, recurred, and one could not now sensibly try to anticipate how humanity would structure their mental life after the abolition of classes, but whatever it would be, it would look nothing like any ideological formation we now knew, not even Communism.[24]

Sidney had had rabbinical training at the Jewish Theological Seminary, and had at one time been attracted by a movement called "Reconstructionist Judaism" (after the title of Dewey's "Reconstruction in Philosophy"). This movement, which Sidney described as "50 percent Moses and 50 percent Dewey," tried to apply pragmatism to traditional Jewish life. Allegorical or metaphorical readings of religious views are always possible, and they have historically flourished. They are also, by their very nature, difficult to control or evaluate. However, many traditional Jewish beliefs presented themselves as if they were true statements of fact, but were clearly false, if you took them that way. To say that they were "true statements of facts" was to claim that they were not just "warrantedly assertable relative to our best existing standards of enquiry," but more than that (although the nature of the surplus ["more than"] was unclear). However, what was "warrantedly assertable" was that god did not really exist, had not made the world, had not chosen and made a covenant with the Jewish people, had not split the Red Sea, had not given Moses any commandments, and so forth. However, the Reconstructionist claimed that even to ask the question whether such beliefs were "true or false" was to miss the point. What was important was that there was a body of traditional beliefs, values, and practices that "worked" for a certain community, gave meaning to their lives, contributed to social cohesion, and fostered progress in human well-being. One didn't even have to commit oneself to saying that these beliefs were "metaphors"; it was just that they had shown themselves to be valuable and to "work" for Jews. To obsess about whether these beliefs were "true" was to remain inappropriately attached to the traditional programme of "true belief." The continued actual flourishing of the Jewish community was all the proof one needed of their value.

There was, however, as Sidney quickly realised, a serious hitch. He found giving sermons difficult. He would start speaking about the way in which God spoke to Moses through the burning bush, but immediately felt the need to interrupt himself. Looking earnestly at the congregation, he would ask "Do you *believe* any of this?" This was not simply Sidney's personal problem. "Believe," after all, can mean a number of different things. First, it can refer to a willingness to affirm certain propositions—that is, "I believe that Tabitha is in the garden" can mean "I (would) affirm that Tabitha is in the garden." Tacitly, I am letting you know that I am perhaps not absolutely, but only reasonably sure about this, and if you would care to use the best available methods (in this case going into the garden to look for yourself), you would see that this assertion is warranted. However, there are other uses of "believe" which put much less emphasis on the explicit affirmation of some proposition, and more on real, especially persistent, focused action. Why does that young man continue to go around trying and failing to sell those newspapers on the street that no one wants to buy? Because he believes in the Party, its programme, and its projects. This might be true although he would not affirm every single point of the Party programme, and might not even be able to formulate, or much care whether he was able to formulate, every particular position the Party took on every issue. Perhaps the Communist Party at some times had this exceptionally high level of expectation of its militants, but the members of the Labour Party who knock on my door in Cambridge do not come near imagining that I could use this criterion for judging them. Here what is paramount is that men or women believe in the Party if they allow themselves to be guided in action (to a large extent) in a certain way. To be sure, there is overwhelming pressure in the direction of connecting these two senses of "belief" as closely as possible: to allow one's action to be guided by beliefs, and only by beliefs that were to a high degree "warrantedly assertable." Pragmatism itself is historically part of this pressure. Nevertheless, the two senses are different, and it seems impossible to imagine that there would not be at least some small space between the two.

Traditionally Jews reserved particular contempt for, and expressed revulsion at, the whole Protestant idea of the primacy of "faith."[25] The whole idea that "faith" somehow "made everything alright" was loathsome and repulsive in itself, but they also rejected it because of the implication that what was most important was the subjective state of the individual. Religion, however, was not about individuals, but about a people, and it was about action, not mental states. Bad actions weren't just cancelled out by changes of heart or by one's attitude; you weren't forgiven for them by having "faith." You weren't supposed to "believe in" (or "have faith in") the God's Law as an individual, but the community was to act according to its dictates. Orthopraxis was infinitely more important than orthodoxy. Provided everyone in the community always did what the Law commanded, individuals could have the most outlandish "personal *beliefs*": someone could try to give names to angels or demons, think the world was going to end next week (or not), hold that the dead rotted into dust, or that all went to a place called *sheol*, or that each was rewarded and punished according to their merit after death, assign numerical values to the letters of the Hebrew alphabet and interpret the results. None of this mattered. Action was governed; speculation was free; and action always had a strong communal component. "Keeping a kosher home" is a different kind of ideal from "accepting Jesus as your personal saviour" (or substitute for this any of the other formulae used in the various Protestant sects).

Because the two senses of belief were not the very same thing, old-fashioned Jews might, perhaps habitually, do various things the Law required without any clear understanding of why, or any particular kind of cognitive belief at all, (and certainly without feeling the need or making any attempt to give a Socratic "account [*logos*] of what they was doing). Given this, one might expect the Jewish community to be ripe for pragmatism.

It turned out not to be so, as Sidney discovered. The practices, rituals, observances, and values did give coherence, order, structure, and meaning to life, but they did so only provided that they were *not* explicitly seen as things to be cultivated *because* they gave meaning and coherence to life. In fact, if you stopped thinking they were embedded in a network of "true" beliefs (in something like the traditional sense of "true"), they lost their power to create or even retain meaning. The practices couldn't maintain themselves autonomously, without appeal to Truth, but that is what pragmatism would have required. If the congregation did not believe in the Truth of some claims, the practices simply failed to function / work effectively as cement for solidarity and meaningfulness, and as lubricant for smooth interaction. So the more that Sidney explained that Jewish beliefs about Moses, Sinai, the Parting of the Red Sea, and so forth were not true (in the traditional sense)—although they were "pragmatically valuable"—and that to expect more was a mistake, the smaller his congregation got. William James spoke of the "will to believe" as operating in cases of religious belief, but here there seems to be something even more archaic, like a "need" of the kind discussed by Feuerbach and Marx:[26] It is as if the members of Sidney's congregation "needed" traditional truth. This, of course, leaves open the question whether they "needed" it in the way in which all humans need water in order to survive or in the way in which a drug addict "needs" his next dose. Was it (to change the religious context) just *pain artisanal,* was it the Bread of Life, or was it the opium of the people that they needed? In principle the dwindling of the congregation could have been the result of some specific deficiencies with Sidney, for instance in his presentation, but that seems unlikely for a number of very good reasons, one of them being that few people were as charismatic as Sidney when he was speaking. If it wasn't Sidney's fault, was it a deficiency of Sidney's congregation—it would have "worked" for some other people? Or was it a problem with Judaism specifically—something about Judaism means that beliefs associated with it need to be held to be true, but that might not be the case with all world views. Finally, maybe it was just a fault of our time and place: in modern, industrial (or capitalist?) societies one could no longer get away with mythic thought, metaphors, or approximations, but one needed something that claimed to be "true" in the full sense. Perhaps, however, that was not the case everywhere and would not remain the case even here in the West forever.

Sidney's experience might be thought to be one further instance of the general truth that "meaning" is sometimes surprisingly impervious to intentional engineering.[27] You can't intentionally create tradition or even re-create or restore it, because the thing about really following a traditional way of life is that you don't know that that is what you are doing. In very many of what we call "traditional ways of life" certain choices do not even arise. Lighting a candle in the room is not "using traditional lighting" when there is no alternative except to sit in the dark (or set fire to the furniture). Only when electric lights are at least conceivable, does lighting a candle become "the traditional way," and then it becomes a possible choice. When doing it "the traditional way" becomes a *choice,* in one sense the tradition has already broken down and one is confronted with a new situation.[28] You certainly are not leading a traditionally meaningful form of life, if you are doing so because someone has *told you* that acting in this way will make your life meaningful. It is one thing to act and not worry too much about what one should believe, or to be satisfied with what are mere phrases: "That's the way we do things." That may be fine, as long as the question of belief and reasons, against a background of possible alternatives, never *really* arises; never arises, as James says, as a "live option."[29] As long as things are vague, or real questions can remain unexpressed or be avoided or people are satisfied with hand-waving or empty platitudes, things may continue. The situation changes completely when questions of belief and reasons for belief are explicitly raised and can't be avoided or finessed. In our society, at any rate after the French Revolution, the idea that one can raise questions about anything has become ubiquitous. Then, to be told that the reason you are to do or continue to do something is not because of anything that happens to be true, but because it "works to give meaning to our lives" will fall flat. You can't be told to be unreflective or to unask questions that have once been asked. Or at the very least success in making questions unasked will require a very considerable amount of extra effort and skill. "Study your Latin" is an injunction that makes sense and can be followed; "Study your Latin *and like it*" doesn't have the same status. You can't successfully set out to be traditionalist. The very fact that you "set out to do it" means you will end up with something different from a traditional life, and will it have the same meaning?

Another way to think about Sidney's experience is that it perhaps shows that "it is warrantedly assertable" and "it works"—two phrases I have been using almost interchangeably as formulations of the central tenet of pragmatism—may have started out close to each other, but they quickly diverge, and when they do so, the intuition behind pragmatism loses its force. In particular, "warranted assertability" comes, in fact, in a modern society, to be closely connected with systematic observation and scientific experiment, whereas "it works," as in the phrase "it works for me" (a usage that did not exist before the late 1960s, but which expresses the central idea of William James's pragmatism very well), has a much wider purview altogether, referring usually to dimensions more closely connected with "undisturbed experience" where that means psychic and emotional comfort.

There was, perhaps, a way of putting the striving for a global world view in a way which made it at least slightly more amenable to prag-

matist appropriation. If, as Dewey and others emphasised, we were
looking for what worked to ensure smooth experience, then surely
that would include a natural propensity to look for more general
rather than more ad hoc solutions. So there were good pragmatist
reasons to universalise. Perhaps trying to fit everything into the
Procrustean bed of a one-size-fits-all Truth was a hindrance to enquiry, but it makes perfect sense to try to simplify life by finding
solutions that would work in a number of different cases, so that
one did not have to face *every* problem *ab ovo* and find a unique
solution, for it. This was also a way of exercising intelligence. It
won't get you to proper, full-blown traditional "truth," but it does
at least show that the search for comprehensiveness, simplicity, and
unity is not just an accident, although it is perhaps then Nietzsche
rather than Dewey who turns out to be most relevant. Human life is
not so much a search for resolving individual encountered problematic situations, but a constant process of moving back and forth
between attempts to get a general and definitive way of dealing
with the world and seeing through any actual construct as deficient, inadequate, and distorting. Seeing through the deficiencies of
the opinions we have formed does not in itself advance us on some
purported road to truth (as Hegel thought). It puts us back more or
less where we have started, but given who we are (weak humans) we
cannot but have another go at the same doomed cycle of illusion,
like a squirrel on a treadmill. Much of Nietzsche's writing is, as it
were, a written transcript of such processes.

This split between the project of replacing "truth" with what is
warrantedly assertible and that of replacing it with what works is perhaps mirrored in a significant difference within the pragmatist
movement itself: the disagreement between Peirce and James about
the doctrine of the "Real Presence" in the Christian sacrament of the
Eucharist. Catholics say and are meant to believe that the bread and
wine in the Christian sacrament of Eucharist are in all empirical ways
just bread and wine, but are also "really" the very body and blood of
Jesus; whereas Protestants characteristically hold that Jesus is not

"really present" in the wine and wafer, but that these are mere symbols, aides-mémoires, and so on. Peirce[30] says that this shows that for the pragmatist there is no difference between what Catholics think and what Protestants think; the purported difference is meaningless and without foundation: after all, they both agree that all scientific experiments will show that the bread and wine are nothing but bread and wine, and that is what counts for the pragmatist. James,[31] however, takes almost exactly the opposite tack: clearly the difference is not meaningless, but rather vital, because accepting the doctrine of the Real Presence means you change your real behaviour significantly. If you are a Catholic, you treat the bread with exaggerated care and respect, you prepare for receiving it in a special way and expect it to have particular effects, you genuflect before the altar if a consecrated host is present. If you are a Protestant, you don't do any of these things and think them superstitions. If you are a Catholic, the doctrine "works" for you, integrating you into a community of the living and the dead, giving your life meaning and orientation, and a very different structure from that one would have as a Protestant. There is a real palpable difference between being a Catholic and being a Protestant. What difference, James says, could be more "pragmatically" significant?

Nietzsche

Sidney's experience with his congregation ought to have caused him to read more Nietzsche, who saw the dilemma he had faced in his Reconstructionist community, I think, very clearly, and who took it very seriously. Sidney thought Nietzsche was just a kind of Neo-Kantian critic of religion and morality with a perspectivist epistemology and, of course, that strand does exist in Nietzsche. However, it coexists with many other strands, some of the most interesting of which are even more deeply incompatible with Kant than perspectivism is. Perhaps he would have said about Nietzsche something like what he often said about the late Wittgenstein: "I see that what he writes is very good philosophy, but it is not my idiom." He was right that philosophy is not just about questions, concepts, and arguments, but is also about idioms. Father Krigler was, as one might have expected given his background, a serious student of Nietzsche. I remember him saying that Nietzsche neatly and succinctly summed up nineteenth- and twentieth-century German philosophy with his poem "Die Krähen schrein" (which I then, of course, immediately learned by heart). Krigler, however, tended to interpret Nietzsche as a warning example of what would happen if one lost one established world view (Christianity in its debased Protestant form ["die Schwundstufe des Christentums"]) and was not able to establish any meaningful contact with the alternative (the socialist movement that eventually gave birth to Communism).

If ancient philosophy was obsessed with the distinction between appearance and reality and the relation between the two, Nietzsche's obsession is subtly different: it is with "appearance" itself and our relation to it; this is what makes him especially relevant. His teacher, Schopenhauer, thought that the world we thought we saw in our waking everyday life was "mere appearance," "insubstantial illusion," part of the "veil of Maya."[32] Things we encounter in the world present themselves as if they were fully substantial and real, but really are not, so we are deceived. When a wise person realises that they are just appearances, he should, Schopenhauer thinks, withdraw his willing from them—why try to embrace, pursue, or realise empty chimaeras? Since *all* is illusion, one should detach the will from *everything;* that is, our will should turn completely against itself into total self-negation. Nietzsche, on the other hand, agrees that what we encounter is not real things-in-themselves but appearances, but he points out that they are correctly called "*mere* appearances" only if they can be contrasted with something else which is not a mere appearance, but which is really real. They are "deceptive" only if we refer or connect them to some purported other "reality." If there is no such thing, it is not clear why we couldn't, if we were strong enough, accept the appearances of the world for what they are, without either being taken in by them or detaching our wills from them. We could perhaps continue to engage with them and affirm them. Schopenhauer's universal negation could, under the appropriate circumstances, mutate into global, unlimited affirmation.

Roughly speaking, then, Schopenhauer thought that human life is a dream (therefore a lie); no one, however, can *accept* that *so one must turn away from it*. Nietzsche, in a memorable phrase from *Geburt der Tragödie,* opposes to this its reversal: "Es [das Leben] ist ein Traum; ich will ihn weiterträumen."[33] A dream is not a lie, it does not deceive me, if I *know* that it is a dream, and do not take it for something it is not. Clearly, we can suspend our tendency to take something that appears to us and try to relate it to something else, called "reality," or we can even stop trying to ask the question of its "truth." We do this all the time in art. The question is whether it is even in principle possible (or "actually possible for us") to adopt this attitude not merely toward some exceptional phenomena, but toward our everyday life as a whole. Can I see my whole life really as having the standing of nothing but a kind of theatrical performance?

Suppose Schopenhauer, who died in 1860, had lived long enough to go to see the premiere of *Tristan* (1865) but stood up in the middle of the first act to shout: "That woman is not a medieval Irish princess, but a Portuguese-Danish opera singer in a funny costume. I'm leaving. I came here to see Isolde and will not be fobbed off with Frau Malwina Schnorr von Carolsfeld. I've been lied to and cheated, and I want my money back!" When he discovers that the management won't give him his money back, he vows to stop going to the theatre at all anymore. Anyone adopting this attitude toward human life in general will quickly discover that there is no management and so a fortiori, no return of the entrance fee and no one to sue for damages or lost opportunity costs. What "opportunities" does one lose by virtue of being born?[34] And in any case, who is so lucky as to have the choice whether or not to be born?

Is there, then, a "need" for a world view, and for a world view that was "true?" There could be at least four reasons for thinking that there was no such need. First one could imagine that there never was and never had been any such need at all. It was all just a simple, if monumental, mistake: perhaps "truth" was a confused or superfluous notion or it made no sense whatever to think one could have a "total" theory of everything of the kind that would be required for a world view. One cannot, it might be argued, be said to have a genuine "need" for something inherently impossible. It is, of course, true that in one sense one cannot have a "need" for something that is inherently impossible, if by "need" one means something without which I cannot survive. It can't be that I cannot survive without owning a square triangle. However, the term "need" is also perfectly legitimately used in a looser sense than this to refer to a deeply rooted striving which will overcome a surprising number of obstacles to move us in one direction rather than another. If it is a real, perhaps even a compulsive, striving, it might well be the case that even knowing it is directed at something which is impossible will not automatically free us of it.

Second, one could think, with Nietzsche, that whether the need existed or not depended on the "strength" of the people involved. Strong people did not have this need; weak people did, and whether one was strong or weak was just a natural fatality or a biological fact of some kind. This in itself certainly did not imply any moral judgment and should be no cause for shame. If you were weak, you would simply feel the need, and there would in fact be little anyone could do to change that; argumentative criticism of the particular world view you adopted might, or might not, cause you to modify or abandon it, but, if so, you would light on another soon enough. The need was like an itch; as long as you were weak and it remained, you would find a way of scratching it, and "argumentation" was beside the point. Maybe only the *Übermensch,* who was by definition no longer human, could fully dispense with "the truth" and fully embrace and affirm a world of appearance. Still, the *Übermensch* might be an ideal we humans could entertain on the path of trying to overcome ourselves.

Third, one could think, with Marx, that whether such a need existed and what particular form it took when it did exist was a social matter, depending on the level of development of the forces of production in society, the existing work relations and the class structure. Just as in a classless society the subjection of the individual to kinds of uniformity required by the demands of production would stop, and the grip of thinking in abstract equivalences (including "labour time" and all forms of justice) would loosen, so the orientation to a purported non-pragmatist "Truth" would gradually decay and disappear and we would be satisfied with what (we know) would work.

Finally, one could hold, with Heidegger, that Being might stop calling to us and demanding of us that we make an image or picture of it. Perhaps if it began to speak to us again and in a different way, it would demand of us not representation, but for us to cultivate and foster it—to be the shepherds, not the photographers or painters of Being. Heidegger, radical anti-Pelagian that he was, thought that the initiative for any such transformation, if it occurred at all, would have to come from Being itself, not from anything we did, although, of course, we might respond to the call, if it was issued, in more or less appropriate ways. As he said at the end of his life: "Nur ein Gott kann uns retten" ["Only a god can save us"].[35]

As I said above, I lost contact with Krigler when he moved so far west as to be outside my ken. One might think that, in parallel to that, I lost touch with Sidney, because I moved so far east (to Cambridge) that our worlds could no longer intersect. That, however, would not be the whole truth. If one thinks that it is a central part of pragmatism to value actions, deeds, real changes, rather than mere words, Sidney had always been a rather odd kind of pragmatist, in that for him the spoken word was *everything*. He could (and did) talk about anything; argue one side of an issue, then change and argue the other, reversing positions immediately, elegantly, and at will; assimilate any new perspective; counter, deflect, or rebut any objection, or accept it and suggest revisions of the original position that had been criticised. He was an absolute master of all of this. It was his

way of keeping the world at a safe distance. You could *say* anything
to him and it was *all* grist for his mill. However, although spoken
words were everything, also, in an odd way, they were *nothing*. They
weren't real, but part of an autonomous realm of discourse, and did
not necessarily lead to deeds or consequences. One could also, when
talking with him, sometimes get the sense of being caught in a web
of words: one could say anything precisely because the words did not
really count; they were mere speech. Sidney and I eventually had a
terminal falling out, ostensibly about the appointment of a new
member to the academic department of which we were both members. He supported the appointment and I opposed it. After a very
long and very acrimonious series of debates, interviews, and discussions in the department and the university, the decision was taken to
make the appointment. This was disappointing, but it was the sort
of thing that happens in human life and which one must deal with
as best one can. The fact that Sidney and I were on opposite sides of
what I took to be an extremely serious matter also did not bother me
terribly—we often disagreed; what could be more usual among philosophers? One might even say it was our natural state, as the joke
had it: two philosophers, three opinions. However, the day after the
final vote, he came up to me and tried to suggest that life would now
simply go on as before; this infuriated me. In my view, this had not
just been one further turn in the argument, that could be countered
or reversed by another dialectical twist, but an actual decision had
been made which had consequence that changed reality. I made the
countersuggestion to him that if he wished things to remain as they
had been, he should write to the provost immediately and say that
we, the members of the department, had not really intended to make
a decision and needed more time for further discussion; *then* life could
continue as before. When he started explaining evasively and inter-
minably why he was not willing to do this, I lost my temper and took
the nuclear option, doing the one thing I knew he would find it difficult to construe as a mere move in a verbal game or which he could
make disappear by verbal redescription: I told him I was not going

to talk to him anymore. If I had been less angry, I might have responded more positively to his no doubt genuine desire that we stay on good terms. Since I am not, and have never been, a Kantian, I never attribute special value to the consistency of action per se; however, since I was able to arrange an almost immediate change in my affiliation to a different academic department, and soon after emigrated to Britain, we never in fact had another conversation. Thus, I don't know, and never will know, whether he actually took the point I was trying to make to him: that speech sometimes has real consequences.

The thing Krigler said that made by far the deepest impression on me was actually something I merely overheard him say when he was speaking with another pupil in the school, a friend of mine who liked to draw. This friend was asking him what he should do if he wanted to become an artist. Krigler was very keen, I knew, on non-representational and non-figurative forms of art. He said to my friend that there was, of course, a discipline involved in art; there were techniques one had to learn, exercises one could do, forms of manual dexterity one had to master, ways of training the eye, established principles of composition. One had to spend the time required to acquire these, or at any rate most of them, but the most important thing if one wanted to become an artist was to set aside half an hour or forty-five minutes a day. During that period, one should ignore completely and forget all the exercises and principles and things one might have learned, and simply take a sheet of paper and draw, even if what one drew was just a squiggle. There was no requirement that what one produced had to *be* good at all, and certainly no requirement that one must *think* or *judge* that it was any good, after one had finished it—in fact, rather the reverse, in that if one was developing one's powers, one's judgment should concomitantly become ever more fastidious and one should become more and more dissatisfied. Nevertheless, at the end of every day one should be able to pick up a sheet of paper and say: "So. **THIS** is what-I-do-on-a-day-like-this." The only way to explain further what "a-day-like-this" meant was to show the drawing. This has always struck me as one of the purest descriptions of the creative urge I have ever encountered.

I have written out what Krigler said in a nonstandard way to try to capture the stress of his voice and his intentions. The full stop after "So" meant, I take it, that my friend should stand back at the end of the day and be prepared, when he looked at his drawing, to be surprised. Nietzsche once claimed that in Homer "Achilles" was best understood as shorthand for an impersonal verbal expression, not as the "name" of a "subject." As it were: "It is now achillesing here" on the model of "it is now raining here"; the purported personal subject was a retrospective invention (*hinzugedichtet*), added for moralising reasons.[36] But for Krigler, when my friend, the beginning artist, looked at the work, the focus was to be on the object that came into existence, the drawing, not on himself as the subject who produced it or indeed on the action out of which it arose. The parallel would be if I were to look at the Cam after a heavy rain and say: "So. **THIS** is the-Cam-on-a-day-like-this." The artist was the channel through which some impersonal energy passed which discharges itself in the real object of attention, the drawing.

What Krigler did *not* say was that when my friend looked at the drawing, he would come to, or should be trying to come to, know himself better, or attain greater understanding of who exactly he was. The formula was not: "So. **I** did-this-on-such-a-day." One could, if one wished, turn this into an exercise in attempting to get self-knowledge, but that was a different project, and one that would distort what should be going on here.

I have said that this seemed to me to describe "the creative urge," but perhaps a better way to put it would be that it says something about individual creativity. For a Catholic, the Holy Ghost is the spirit of creativity, but the Ghost is essentially realised in this life as the spirit of a community, not as the psychological state of an isolated individual. It descends on groups assembled in certain ways and for certain purposes. Individuals may be the vehicles of certain actions, but only as members of such an appropriately constituted community. No major medieval cathedral had a single architect, although, of course, without the imaginative and the physical labour of generations of individuals, none would exist. As Hegel pointed out, "spirit" is neither a purely individual nor an entirely collective phenomenon, but rather "An I that is a We and a We that is an I," a point also fully accepted by reflective Communists.[37]

It has been said that those who have neither art nor science need religion,[38] just as those who have no character need "principles." This immediately raises the question: "What is it, the lack of which requires one to have 'character?'"—a question to which I have no answer. Certainly, the philosophy which gives the central place to "having principles" is the natural dogma of bureaucrats, civil servants, and accountants; as the philosopher Friedrich Schiller put it in the late eighteenth century, it is a doctrine for the servants, not the children of the house.[39] Perhaps then one should reverse the usual perspective on world views. The usual view is that any distinct community will have a distinct world view, and, of course, if one takes the term "world view" sufficiently broadly and allows it to be sufficiently indeterminate and inexplicit, this will be right. Members of the same community will often have much in common, many habits, attitudes, reactions, ways of doing things, beliefs; however, it obviously does not follow from this that they share a single determinate, well-defined, explicit set of organised beliefs about the world. First of all, much of the communality may be constituted by aspects of human action of which the members of the community are not explicitly aware and which are not loosely connected with particular beliefs. Second, if they have "shared beliefs," these might form a collection of overlapping sets rather than one world view. Third, many of the beliefs one might be tempted to say they "shared" will be inherently indeterminate in content, and this may be a positive thing in any number of ways. Early Christians all thought Jesus was the Saviour,[40] but this seeming agreement actually masked enormous differences in the way they construed what that meant—indeed if they gave much thought at all to what it meant. The history of Christianity has been one in which ecclesiastical powers have tried to control the writing of history, imposing on the early days of the Church a scheme of "orthodoxy" (defined ex post by what the great Ecumenical Councils of the third century agreed on) versus heresy, projecting this distinction back onto the past where it clearly had no real place. Perhaps it is precisely when genuine communal energies begin to dry up or when disciplinary demands are given priority over all else that the need for a "world view" in a stricter sense becomes keener. Similarly, it is perhaps those whose community is diseased, especially threatened, moribund, or in steep decline at the end of a period of great vitality who need a world view. Hegel analysed very sharply the illusion that consisted in thinking that by formulating a philosophical picture of the world one could restore a community to vibrancy. A world view is like a black-and-white photo of a painting by Delacroix or Grunewald, which by its very nature could never restore or refresh the colours of the original.[41]

None of the many philosophers I met later in life, despite the evident intellectual power and seriousness many of them had, had nearly the real, continuing effect on me that Béla and Sidney did. In his *Apology* Plato's Socrates imagines the pleasure he would find if after death there really were an afterlife: how many interesting people he could talk with![42] I have also had this fantasy of meeting again with my two teachers. We might even form a discussion club with a snappy name like "The Lev-Bronstein / Leon-Trotsky-Memorial (Reconstructionist) *Minyan* (*in spe*) and Sodality of St. Jude, Patron of Hopeless Cases." Of course, we would need at least another seven members to get the canonical minimal number. Whom else could we invite to join us? However, even if, contrary to everything that reason tells us, there is such a thing as human activity, or even life, after biological death, the words spoken there would be entirely without real consequences, and so how could they not be empty? If so, why imagine that such an existence would have room for anything like religious rituals or for philosophical discussion?

2

Games and Proverbs

There is a well-known painting by the sixteenth-century Flemish painter Pieter Bruegel (called "The Elder"), now in the Kunsthistorisches Museum in Vienna, which shows children playing various games in the streets of a village.[1] Over a hundred children are depicted on the panel, engaged in a wide variety of games; experts can, it seems, distinguish at least eighty different pastimes (Figure 2.1). The picture is like that of a number of others by Bruegel in that it is crowded with different figures actively engaged in some activity, not merely, for instance, posing for a formal portrait. Others like this include *The Massacre of the Innocents* (also in the Kunsthistorisches Museum), *The Contest between Carnival and Lent* (also in the KM), and *Netherlandish Proverbs* (Figure 2.2) (in Berlin). At first glance, many of these panels can seem almost claustrophobic, too full of people, too cluttered with chaotic details, or even too much lacking in a simple visual structure and surveyable order—very much, that is, like real human life, and thus repellent.

For an eye accustomed to High Renaissance Italian painting, one can see how the lack of simple symmetry in many of Bruegel's paintings might constitute a serious obstacle to appreciation. Take as an example of Italian Renaissance art at its best Raphael's fresco *School of Athens* (Figure 2.3) in the Vatican. Just as is the case with the paint-

2.1 Pieter Bruegel the Elder, *Children's Games*. Kunsthistorisches Museum /
Wikimedia Commons

ings by Bruegel mentioned above, Raphael's fresco represents a large
number of individual figures, over twenty, but, in contrast to Bruegel,
it shows extreme single point perspective. All the architectural details—for instance, the nested sequence of arches—reinforce the
focus of the eye on the pair of philosophers in the middle—Plato and
Aristotle—with the other figures, representatives of other philosophical schools, grouped on both sides of that central pair in a way that
emphasises their importance. The line formed by the figures of these
philosophers, all lined up in a row on each side of Plato and Aristotle, makes two lovely sinuous curves on both sides of the picture.
One figure, to be sure, Diogenes the Cynic, sits—actually he seems
to perch uncomfortably—by himself on the steps; he is not a member
of the party of Plato (the "idealists" or "spiritualists") on the left, or

2.2 Pieter Bruegel the Elder, *Netherlandish Proverbs*. Gemäldegalerie / Wikimedia Commons

the party of Aristotle (the "realists," or perhaps "naturalists") on the right, and he is marked out by his spatial location as the exception. Even a painting by Bruegel that has roughly the same binary, right / left, contrastive structure has a strikingly different structure. Take *The Battle between Carnival and Lent*. In this painting there are two prominent figures representing the two times of year, and two modes of living. In the bottom foreground an overweight Sir Carnival in a blue jerkin mounted on a tun is jousting with an emaciated Lady Lent seated on a kind of primitive trolley and wielding a long stick with a flattened end on which two fish have been placed. These two figures, however, are not in the absolute centre of the painting, and Sir Carnival is placed slightly higher than Lady Lent, as if (still) dominating her. If, in the painting by Raphael, the two because I can walk down the corridor in the *Kunsthistorisches Museum,* out of the room with the Bruegels and look at a Titian or a Velàzquez, or even cross a few streets to see the Klimts in another museum, or come home and go to see one of my favourite Iranian bowls in the Fitzwilliam, or, for that matter, look at the metal bust of Lenin (signed 'СК ЗАВАЛОВ') on the shelf in my study. And, to top it all, I am not (yet) dead, as Bruegel is." It is not right to say that this attitude is a way of keeping art morally at a distance; rather it is a particularly morally self-serving mode of appropriation.

Some people have felt great attraction to Nietzsche's injunction to make one's life a work of art. Many of them have interpreted this injunction to mean that I should make my life unique in the way in which a work of art, they think, is unique. This would mean that my life should not just be an instance of a certain given type of life. It should at least aspire to be "incomparable." This might seem problematic for at least two reasons. First, "works of art" are *not* actually absolutely unique; that is, they are not "incomparable" to anything else,[4] just as my life is not "incomparable" but can easily be compared in various ways to the lives of other people my age, with my background, my resources and my infirmities. Artworks create and occupy a distinct space of their own—if we don't know it is a play, we should be tempted to intervene and save Caesar from Cassius and Brutus—but they belong to recognisable types (dance, sculpture, film, literature) and to distinct genres (epic, lyric, comedy). Nietzsche himself was explicit about this and throughout his life obsessed with the differences between different kinds of art and especially different genres of literature. If this is the case, what kind of work of art can my life be? Why make the unmotivated leap from "work of art" to "narrative" (that is, a *literary* work of a particular kind)? Why not turn my life into a statue or an image, a building, a dance, or a work of music? Why can't my life be best represented in the lyric rather than the narrative mode? There may be legal and policing reasons for this. Thus, narrative, one might think, lends itself more easily as a mode of presentation of self to use in a court of law than lyric does.

2.3 Raphael, *School of Athens.* Vatican Museums / Wikimedia Commons

central figures of Plato and Aristotle seem to impose order on the gracefully organised company of their acolytes, in *The Battle between Carnival and Lent* the other figures in the painting—those, that is, apart from Sir Carnival and Lord Lent themselves—are not unitarily grouped at all: they seem to have made themselves independent and are pursuing their own different activities: dicing, whipping tops, giving alms to mendicants, gutting fish, dancing rounds. All of this without much reference to the two central figures.

In very many of Bruegel's paintings, the "main" actor or action, as given by the title and the associated implicit narrative, is not located anywhere near the centre of the painting at all. In the *Suicide of Saul,* the suicide itself is on a tiny, isolated plateau on the left, while the rest of the painting is dominated by a huge flow of marching armies in a mountainous landscape. In *The Conversion of Saul* and *Christ Carrying the Cross* the central figure is dwarfed by the surrounding crowds so that even finding him is like looking for a needle in a haystack. In the most well-known example, cited in the famous poem by Auden,[2] the body of "Icarus" is not even visible in *The Fall of Icarus;* one must look carefully at the bottom right to see two legs protruding out of the water. This decentring of the painting vis-à-vis narrative expectations seems too systematic to be completely accidental. This view of the world is systematically eccentric. It is the view of an individual who doesn't know the story being told.

This tendency toward dissolution of the sense of a centre seems to reach a high point in *Children's Games* and *Netherlandish Proverbs.* There does not even seem to be any central figure, group, or action, hidden or not, in *Children's Games.* Different individual children and groups of children play *different* games in different parts of the canvas. Some of these games may well have definite rules, like the game of tossing hats depicted in the lower right-hand side; others, like the boy climbing the tree in the upper-left corner, do not. "Climbing a tree" has "rules" only in at best a Pickwickian sense ("Do not fall off," but even falling off can be part of the fun, if "correctly" done). Space is locally organised (and the individual games are locally meaningful and, if there are rules at all, they are local rules): the children playing hoops or bowls do not impinge on those walking on stilts or swimming in the river, and if there are rules for swimming they are different from the rules of playing bowls. The different games are certainly not part of a unitary *Gesamtkinderspiel.* Similarly, the Berlin painting about proverbs depicts the *different* contexts in which each proverb becomes meaningful and applicable. The soldier in full armour who is putting a bell around the cat's neck may just as well be construed as existing in a different space from the man confessing to the devil behind a pillar for all the interaction there is between them (none), and although the man with the cat is sitting on top of the very same wall against which another man in a breastplate is knocking his head, the two of them seem to have no cognisance of each other.

One can think of *Children's Games* and *Netherlandish Proverbs* as works that comment on human social life, which, of course, is a statement one can make without any necessary reference to the psychological intention of the painter, about which we know in fact virtually nothing. That, however, does not matter. At the moment of writing (June 2019), *Children's Games* seems a very apt image of the British political class in their attempt to negotiate Brexit: no adults visible, just a chaotic collection of tiny people pursuing, in small groups and as individuals, their own autistic goals, although obviously Bruegel in the sixteenth century couldn't have intended exactl this association. *Netherlandish Proverbs* gives a more sinister view; the children's game are mostly harmless, if pointless (the little gi whirling around in the upper-left corner), most of the sayings illu trate either the active folly, the ignorance, or the malice of huma If some of the games are minimally sociable, the proverbs seem, exclusively, but on the whole to apply to individuals: "*The fool s on the world*" (left toward the top) immediately makes one thin an individual, like Trump; the soldier knocking his head usele against the brick wall (Cheney or Rumsfeld), even "lighting can for the devil" (Blair kneeling before Bush) focuses on the folly o kneeling human figure. If these paintings are representations of world," of "us," then it also seems unavoidable to ask "Where in this painting? Which proverb applies to *me?*" There is, of c a quick answer, which is, however, not very helpful, and, I thin morally rather outrageous, which is: "None of that is *me*, ma the *observer,* the *viewer,* the (ideal) spectator, not a figure painting. If anything, I am 'in' this painting in the way that B himself, the artist who painted it, is."[3] A very comfortable p for me, then, partner and collaborator with genius (Bruegel), plicated in what is seen: "My life, oh no, cannot be summe the way Blair's can be as 'lighting candles for the devil' or in a simple formula or image. I can't even be identified and tied the teeming productivity of Bruegel himself, fecund as he productive of such a profusion of images in dozens of p

If this is a fact, it would seem to be a sociological fact about our form of society. Should I, however, allow my conception of myself, rather than merely my external actions, to be guided exclusively by the demands of public order? Many, of course, have held that thoughts are not, and ought not to be, free: arguably the Plato of the *Republic* and *The Laws*. Certainly in the *Republic* Plato assumes a parallelism between the structure of the soul and public order, and if he thinks that it is the soul that is primary and that the political sphere should mirror the harmony of the well-balanced soul, others might well think the opposite. If one does believe that legal considerations should finally determine my relation to myself, one should at least affirm this clearly and try to think about its consequences.

The second question Nietzsche's injunction raises concerns the notion of "making," that is, of "making one's life" one thing or other. This idea is tempting only if one can distinguish between "making one's life [*something*]" and "just being / acting / living," where "making" is an intentional activity. Actually, this looks very much like a point which is the exact opposite of the one Nietzsche usually makes. In general, Nietzsche seems to wish to emphasise the importance of giving as free rein as possible to the instinctual element in human life as opposed to the more reflective or conscious side. "Living out your instincts," however, would seem to be something rather different from intentionally making anything, even "making one's life a work of art." In some cases, one can distinguish simply living one's life from "making of one's life a work of art." For instance, Alexander of Macedon was said to have kept a copy of the *Iliad* near his bed,[5] and wanted to make his life *like* that of Achilles (except more so, by surpassing him in deeds of heroism). Achilles, one might imagine, was not in the same way trying to do that: he was not trying to make his life (something), but *living:* trying to take Troy or humiliate Agamemnon or avenge the death of Patroclus, but that is a different thing. "Making one's life (something)" seems to have a strong reflective moment which is lacking in instinctive activity. In making my life something I am consciously taking stock of what it is and trying to change that existing state, transforming it intentionally in one direction (rather than the various other directions in which it could possible evolve). If that is the case, then, looking more carefully at Achilles, he seems less different from Alexander than one might at first imagine. When he is not in battle, we see Achilles sitting beside his tent, himself singing the praises of heroes of old (IX. 185ff.), and we know that his mother, the sea nymph Thetis, has told him that he has a choice between a long, comfortable, but obscure life or a short life of undying glory (IX. 410ff.). We see him reflecting on which he will choose. Which one of the two proposed lives is he going to make his? Finally, of course, he comes to Troy, it seems, with a kind of tutor (IX. 440ff.), Phoenix, who was supposed to teach him how to turn himself into a good speaker of words and doer of deeds. So, Achilles had models for aspiration, and not even for him does it all come absolutely "naturally." This is true despite Nietzsche's fantasies (or, to put it more sympathetically, "philosophical constructions") in *Zur Genealogie der Moral,* about an aboriginal groups of "Masters" who simply didn't think about themselves at all or mould themselves into a shape imposed by reflection at all, who were not even, in any interesting sense "subjects," but were, as it were, sheer act, *all* verb. This, however, is not a realistic description of a way of life that is at all cognitively accessible to us, no matter how far back we reach in the written record. It is, if anything, even less practically accessible to us.

Let's assume then, for the sake of argument, that the model for making one's life a work of art is not the mythic, fully spontaneous, instinct-driven artist, but something that has at least a place for looking before one leaps, and observing where one is intending to leap from. So the painter does not simply push forward, applying colours to a board, panel, wall, or canvas, but in some sense registers what is already there—first the substratum, then gradually the accumulated paint on it—and takes account of that in some process that is like reflection or ratiocination, when proceeding, even if this process is not fully discursive.

As Lessing pointed out, visual arts, as arrangements in space, have to struggle to accommodate representations of change, development, history.[6] To be sure, although the final painting, certainly one "finished" in the sense in which this was understood until the very end of the nineteenth century, was supposed to stand on its own, and certainly not flaunt the marks left by the process of its production—the heavy weather made during Whistler's court case about the fact that his painting did not look "finished" shows this rather clearly[7]—one could, I suppose, interpret Nietzsche's remark about making one's life a work of art as referring to the process of artistic production, rather than the finished product. In most cases, to be sure, there would still be an important difference in that in the case of painting, the artist, in general, makes the work by acting in various ways through time, but there is some final product at the end which has some at least relative stability and can be viewed, by others, and by the artist him- or herself. The finished painting was supposed to last longer than the time needed to paint it. Even cases like Banksy's drawing that shreds itself upon being purchased are clearly individual violations of this expectation, and are intended to be seen as such so they, perhaps paradoxically, work partly by drawing attention to this rule. This isn't the case with a human life: I work on it *and then, at the very moment at which it is complete, I am missing.* There is no product, except perhaps in the imagination of other people who remember me after I am gone, or the perception of gods who see my life as a whole including its very, very end. There are traces of this kind of view in Nietzsche's early work *Die Geburt der Tragödie* when he talks about the Greek gods as the spectators and humans as actors who put on a play for their entertainment. If, however, there are no gods as universal connoisseurs of human lives, is it Achilles who makes his life a work or art or Homer? Themistocles or Herodotus and Plutarch? This would make any project of making my life a work of art oddly dependent on others and their reactions to it. This would be something that was deeply and radically out of my control, which might be a perfectly fair comment in general on human life, but is not what would seem to have been intended by those who speak of making one's life a work of art.

I assume that the basic idea was that I was supposed to be both the artist and the audience of my own life. At *any* given time, though, "my life" will have to be given to me in three parts: a past I remember, a present I perceive, and a future I anticipate. The moment of "anticipation" is essential because if I have no anticipation I have no future, and if I have no future I am dead, so there is no artist, but also no audience. Part of what I have to do if I wish to make my life a work of art is to integrate some remembrance of my past, cognisance of my present, and some minimal proleptic anticipation of what is about to be. The anticipation of the future is crucial. Much of the poignancy of the final words of that most marvellous of the Roman Emperors, the matricidal, anti-Christian Nero, "*Qualis artifex perdeo,*" is that with the artist in one sense that work of art, which is his living human life, perishes, although perhaps another *different* work becomes possible in the form of the images of Nero produced by others, including later writers.

No future, no life-as-a-work-of-art; the role of prolepsis in art cannot be overemphasised. A painter, while at work, presumably sees the present state of the canvas, but also has *some* conception of that-which-is-not-(yet)-there: some idea of an envisaged finished product or at any rate a direction in which he or she wishes to continue. This means a kind of cognitive state that is temporally extended in two senses. First, the painter has a shifting knowledge which is modified during the course of production, if only because with each stroke made, the object, the painting, is changed. Second, at each point he or she has some intentionally and voluntatively tinged apprehension of what he or she is about to do, the stroke that is about to come, the shape that is about to emerge, what "ought to be (but is not yet) there." I fully take the point that this is a significant simplification, also that this is not fully informative in that it doesn't say what *kind,* or kinds, of "knowledge, apprehension, cognisance, (and so forth)" are involved. Finally, I take the point that this account probably overintellectualises what is going on. Whether or not that is the case depends, of course, on what particular account one can give of different kinds of knowledge, and since no such analysis of this is given here, some degree of scepticism and dissatisfaction is appropriate. However, unless one wants to adopt the Nietzschean position that the artist, or at any rate some kinds of artists sometimes, are, in their work, not even in any relevant sense real subjects holding beliefs at all, but just pure outpourings of instinct, unmodified by any form of reflection, thought, or cognition, then something like the account just given would have to hold.

I have spoken of the painter's relation to present perception and to imagined futures, but what about the past? At some level one might argue that just as there is no meaningful perception of the present without at least minimal protentive apprehension of possible futures, so also there would be no cognisance of what is present to me at the moment without the activation of various forms of memory. Still the painter in a medium like oils can effectively cancel the relevant past of the painting, for instance by scraping it off and painting over it, rendering it invisible to the sort of eye (the unaided, or only minimally corrected, human eye) for which the painting is intended. That past doesn't exist, except perhaps, sometimes, for a modern expert equipped with highly specialised technical instruments.

This, I take it, is the second of the two important ways in which the working on a painting is different from living a life. The first has already been mentioned and is a staple in the "existentialist" literature: my own life as lived is *always* incomplete, because when it is "finished," it is over, and, although perhaps an object of contemplation for others, no longer "my life as lived." This refers to the future: to live is to have a future that is not closed and finished, and if one has no future, one is not living. This second aspect of difference has to do with the past. In painting, one can effectively undo the past by removing and painting over it. In human life, my actions have consequences for others; some of them are registered in the public realm or in the memory of others, and, although I may succeed in reinterpreting them, I cannot simply make them disappear at will. If I snub you by acting, under appropriate circumstances, as if you do not exist, I may eventually genuinely forget that I have done that. The fact that I don't remember it does not mean that it necessarily has somehow ceased to exist. You may, for instance, remember it. The Christian hopes, of course, that through a certain kind of religious faith the past can be made *as-if* undone in the limited sense that some of the consequences that are concomitants of past action are no longer associated with it (especially divine punishment), but even this does not actually undo the acts. It, too, merely reinterprets them, putting them in a wider context as part of the prehistory of the salvation of a sinful human individual through divine grace. This line of thought gives prominence to the limitation and faultiness of human memory. The painter can in principle have a terribly poor memory, forgetting, in the course of work, the original project, the bits that are painted over and invisible, and simply getting on from where the painting stands to where it is *now* envisaged as aspiring to be. Perhaps this is not the absolutely highest form of artistic activity, but one can get a finished result from it. In the case of my life, if I am trying to think about it as a whole in order then to make of it a work of art, I am dealing in memory with a constantly whimsically decaying material; that is, with a constantly changing content, parts of which are always sinking into oblivion. I don't remember everything. There is my past as it is documented in historical records and the memory of others, and there is what I remember of it. These two things will invariably diverge. In lots of ethical contexts this divergence is anything but negligible: " I didn't know I was doing that" (when I was doing it) may in some cases be exculpatory; "I don't *remember* doing that," even if this is perfectly true, does not have the same force. That you don't even *remember* having done X to Y may be an additional aggravation of the original offence.

We know well about the "wilful" (or half-wilful) mechanisms for suppression of uncomfortable memories, but even apart from moti-

vated distortions and forms of forgetting, there is simple malfunction. Perspectival recollection and limitation in the registration of details are perhaps not exactly even forms of malfunctioning—because
they are a normal part of the functioning of anything like human
memory. Freud is clearly right that there can be things lodged in the
soul in the past, which we do not remember and which may influence
us in various ways. *Some* things can thus be retained, and, therefore,
perhaps anything *might* potentially be retained. One should not, however, infer from this that *every* impression we ever had is correctly and
vividly retained in all its details "somewhere" in the mind. To assume
this would be to give to the functioning of the human (unconscious?)
mind a perfection and a retentive capacity far beyond anything we
have any reason to attribute to it. Even less should we assume that
every reaction any other person with whom we had dealings, and the
possible offence they may have taken at our actions, is retained somewhere in *our* memory. As long as I am alive, my future is to some extent open and indeterminate, only accessible to me through speculation and planning, but equally my past is a constantly crumbling
papyrus, on which a full text was never written and to which, in
memory, I have only partial and perspectivally skewed access.

So, to pursue the analogy, if I am trying to make my life a work
of art, like, say, one of these Bruegel paintings, I am watching the
panel on which *Children's Games* is taking shape, while knowing that
I shall never see the final, finished version—that will come into being
at the time of my death, when I will no longer be around to see it. I
also know that as I am painting, part of the existing panel is crumbling under my very eyes and hands, as my memory of the past functions in its normal way, retaining only *part* of what is there.[8] Finally,
I know that a viewer who is not me, even now, but certainly after my
death, will, if sufficiently interested to observe my life with concen-
tration, clearly see things there that are invisible to me now, but are
part of the painting, or, at any rate, part of the process by which the
painting came into existence. An external viewer may see parts of the
painting that have already crumbled, or material which has ceased

to exist for me, but is not really either gone or invisible to an outside observer.

One might claim that Bruegel has organised the unitary aesthetic space within the frame of each picture, so he has imposed some unity. This may be true, but Bruegel is still not one of the children playing and his painting is not the same thing as playing hoops or bowls, walking on stilts, or climbing trees nor itself, except accidentally, an illustration of a Dutch proverb. Maybe if I do look at my own life (or my soul), my past, my present, and my future without imposing on it the philosophical construct of a "unified totality," I will see something like the contents of these paintings. Traditional philosophers used a number of different images to speak of the structure of a human life as a whole, or its essential features, or to provide an ideal to be aspired to. There is the Cartesian Narcissus contemplating himself in the pool, or watching the figures move across the stage in the theatre of his mind, or peeping out of his darkened mental chamber through to two tiny sockets of the human eyes into the bright light of the world. There is the Kantian legislator producing and exemplifying in his action a particularly unitary, consistent, and surveyable *Code Napoléon.*[9] There is Plato's ascent to the vision of the Idea of the Good or the medieval *itinerarium mentis ad deum;* there is Wilhelm Meister finally encountering the members of the *Turm-Gesellschaft.* My life is more like *Children's Games* or *Netherlandish Proverbs,* or perhaps, more exactly, like the history of these paintings from the moment Bruegel began to sketch in the very first figures, to the moment, sometime in the future when the last figures become effaced and the panel rots away. My awareness of my own life is a series of flickering moments, located in various of the personages in the panel and, very occasionally, incorporating the imagined perspective in a fictional observer (including, possibly, Bruegel himself, as I imagine him to have been at various points during the production of the picture). Even this is an imaginary projection of mine at a certain point in time. There is no point, not even an imaginary one, from which *all* of this looks like a single, unitary anything.

3

Enlightenment, Genealogy, and the Historicality of Concepts

Sie fragen mich, was alles Idiosynkrasie bei Philosophen
ist? . . . Zum Beispiel ihr Mangel an historischem Sinn, ihr
Haß gegen die Vorstellung selbst des Werdens, ihr Ägyptismus.
Sie glauben einer Sache *Ehre* anzutun, wenn sie dieselbe enthistorisieren, sub specie aeterni—wenn sie aus ihr eine Mumie
machen.

(Nietzsche, *Götzendämmerung*)

The eighteenth century produced a number of important works of
history that can be counted as belonging to the "Enlightenment,"
such as Gibbon's *Decline and Fall of the Roman Empire* (1776–1789).
Still "enlightenment" and "historicisation" do not seem to be natural
bedfellows but rather to be in tension one with the other. What was
most characteristic of the Enlightenment, one might argue, were not
"historicising" discussions, but grand speculative projects, like those
of Condorcet or Kant, which, while they might claim to describe
macro-structures or large-scale patterns in past and present, did not
actually contain much of what we now would call "real history."
Rather, they were attempts to reduce real history to some kind of
schema. After all, the major figures of the Enlightenment were
strongly fixated on an abstract and purportedly universal concept of
"reason," which, to put it mildly, is not the best point of departure

for an understanding of the past or of historical processes. Is it possible that in this respect, as Adorno and Horkheimer claimed, the Enlightenment needed to be enlightened about itself?[1]

In his essay on Kant's article "Was ist Aufklärung?,"[2] Michel Foucault distinguishes between what he calls the "ethos" and what he calls the "dogma" of the Enlightenment. To be an "enlightened person" was a form of life with appropriate habits of thought and action, dispositions, and personality traits. The *"philosophe,"* the quintessential figure of Enlightenment society, was supposed to be relentlessly "critical" in all domains of life; he (or she) was to be an indefatigable enemy of prejudice, rigid dogma, and obsolete tradition, and was never supposed simply to accept the word of any purported "authority" at face value without citing it to appear before the Tribunal of Reason and subjecting it to implacable scrutiny. The major thinkers of the Enlightenment were always critics of their own time: "L'Aufklärung n'est pas [constituée par] la fidelité à des éléments de doctrine, mais plutôt [par] la réactivation permanente d'une attitude: c'est-à-dire d'un êthos philosophique qu'on pourrait caractériser comme critique permanente de notre être historique" [The fidelity to certain elements of doctrine is not what constitutes the "Aufklärung"; rather it is the constant activation of an attitude, that is of a philosophical ethos which one might describe as being that of a permanent critique of our historical being] (Foucault, vol. 4, p. 571).[3] This is one of the reasons the Enlightenment produced so many and such varied programmes for reform of the state, the church, society, the educational system, and science in the second half of the eighteenth century.

It is hard, if not impossible, to deny that the major figures of the Enlightenment, contrary to their own self-conception, and despite their best efforts, were themselves caught up inextricably in "dogmas" of their own. The "cult of the goddess Reason" which was propagated by the Hébertists in the second year of the revolution, was not just a weird and slightly ludicrous singularity, but it was an authentic, if exaggerated, expression of a central motif of the Enlightenment. It is in fact the case that the conception of "reason" to which many of the major figures in the Enlightenment were most attached, was almost as inflexible and dogmatic as the theological doctrines of the established churches which they vigorously rejected: "Reason," they thought, was absolutely universal, unitary, unvarying in space and time, and irresistible, and it gave one a clear and certain criterion for judging any situation, action, desire, belief, practice, or institution whatever. Reason was the opposite of "prejudice," so there was a certain plausibility in the claim that Hans-Georg Gadamer made in the 1960s that the philosophers of the Enlightenment were inconsistent, because they had a prejudice against prejudice.[4]

Foucault is broadly sympathetic to many aspects of this line of criticism of the dogmatism of the Enlightenment. Nevertheless, he is of the opinion that it is both possible and advisable to distinguish these dogmas from something else which it is important to continue to cultivate. This is what he calls the "ethos" of the Enlightenment: the commitment to universal criticism. To remain true to this ethos means that one does not exempt the concepts on which the Enlightenment project itself rests—such concepts as reason, science, knowledge, and truth—from a scrutiny directed at trying to see what authority they have. It is a sign of the seriousness with which Kant took the Enlightenment project that in his *Critiques* he undertook to conduct this scrutiny. This is true, even though the actual results of Kant's enquiry are meagre and disappointing. It is no great surprise that "pure reason" certifies the validity (within certain limits) of its own utterances: when the accused is also at the same time the judge and the jury in his own case, he can look forward with some optimism to the verdict. Is it, however, incontravertibly obvious that "reason" is the only possible judge in matters concerning the authority and justification of beliefs, actions, practices, and institutions? Certainly, some revolutionaries, and not only revolutionaries, have claimed that "history" (itself) was the final court of appeal.[5] They have spoken as if there was a "tribunal of history" to which the Kantian "tribune of reason" is (finally) subordinate. Or should our knowledge of history lead us to the conclusion that the whole conception of a final and ultimate, authoritative tribunal should be dispensed with or relativised? Perhaps the very idea that life is to be construed as the object of permanent proceedings in a court is distorted, incorrect, or wrongheaded. Perhaps the Enlightenment was mistaken to jump to the conclusion that life was like a continuing court case, in which it was imperative to come, quickly and efficiently, to definitive judgments about what was "true" and what "false"; what was "legitimate" and what "illegitimate"; and what was "justified" and what "not justified." We know that many people find it difficult psychologically to tolerate even for short periods of time ambiguity, indeterminacy, and anything that renders boundaries indistinct or straddles them. This human trait can take a number of particular, historically variable forms and can be weaker or stronger at different times and in different places.[6] It is a definitive deficiency of the Enlightenment that it exhibited this weakness to a rather high degree, and even gloried in it, rather than recognising it for what it was.

Foucault wishes to cultivate the "ethos of enlightenment," the commitment to continuing critique, but without acceding to the "blackmail" ("*chantage*") often exercised by those who insist that this ethos requires adopting certain particular eighteenth-century dogmas: "On doit échapper à l'alternative du dehors et du dedans; il faut être aux frontières." This means, roughly, "We need to try to escape the alternative 'inside (the strictly drawn boundaries of Enlightenment Reason) *or* outside,' and we must learn to live on the boundary itself." How, though, is one to conduct a court if *all* the relevant frontiers and lines of demarcation between events, actions, and concepts are fluid, that is, if we take history seriously?

It is a well-known fact that "critique" originally meant "analysis," not, as it has come to mean in many cases today, "rejection," or "opposition." To "criticise" a position meant to take it apart and try to understand it, rather than (necessarily) to argue against it and reject it. So the "critical attitude" which is the central component in the ethos of the Enlightenment is not one of negativism, but merely of putting into abeyance forms of automatic belief. It means keeping one's cognitive and affective distance from existing institutions, practices, and beliefs, and maintaining one's faculties of analysis and judgment in good shape, in order the better to be able to understand and evaluate one's surroundings and one's world. There is a venerable philosophical precedent for this demand for suspension, in the interests of clarity and mental hygiene, of our automatic identification with the social world in which we live. The ancient sceptics were not committed to rejecting all the views other philosophers presented, but, rather, they simply wanted to consider and investigate them carefully, and the arguments for and against them, before making any judgment. That the arguments offered don't have the force attributed to them by those who propound them, and therefore do not amount to a conclusive reason to accept the view being propagated, is not the fault of the sceptic.[7] Suspending judgment in such cases is not perverse, but perfectly reasonable, and that this outcome results again and again, is also, for the sceptic, just a fact to be observed, not something from which he draws any theoretical conclusions.

As a good *philosophe* that is a *self*-critical partisan of the Enlightenment, one should allow oneself to ask the question which Kant never seriously raises: Is there such a thing as *"pure"* Reason? That is, is there a human capacity to generate its own substantive concepts which are clear, well-defined, and can be abstracted from the historical and linguistic context in which they have their final origin, so as to permit "reason itself," in employing them, to be a judge of the kind Kant envisages in a tribunal of universal competence and jurisdiction. Kant's austere "High Justicer" may turn out, on inspection, to be the cleaning lady of the halls, laboratories, and libraries of science, or a mere "underlabourer" in the work gang directed by the leaders of one political grouping or another. Hegel's utterly devastating criticism of Kant's ethics, and in particular of the view that the principle of non-contradiction could give one an adequate criterion for morality, means that appeals to "pure Reason" alone will not really advance us at all in morality, science, and politics.

The Enlightenment developed a huge apparatus for evaluating and judging opinions, beliefs, and claims to authority. It is possible, following the lead of Husserl, to "put brackets around" the claims to validity that are made by this huge and complex machine, in order to investigate it. Doing this will reveal internal structural features of the system and also ways in which it is connected to the rest of society, which are otherwise hard to see. How and why do people in society come to make certain statements, and why do some of these become firmly established as recognised "truths" whereas others that are in principle equally possible either never get formulated or are immediately excluded from further discussion or even suppressed? There is a simple answer to this: the ones that establish themselves are always those that "correspond to reality," whereas the ones that do not get discussed are ignored because they do not so correspond. This answer, however, is not either in itself plausible, nor does it seem to conform at all to what we know about history. The same is true for the variant of this answer that is specifically characteristic of Enlightenment thinkers: "The statements and opinions that are 'rational' are widely discussed, and will eventually be accepted; others are not and will not be." A historian, for instance, might legitimately be interested in the Christian doctrine of the Trinity, a complex set of beliefs that was exceedingly important for more than a thousand years in the West. Such a historian might examine the prehistory of various of the elements that come to make up that doctrine, the various versions of henotheism and monotheism that were part of the late-ancient milieu in which the doctrine gradually crystalised, and various attempts to put some of these elements together in differing ways. One might ask how theologians in Alexandria, Antioch, Constantinople, and elsewhere came to know these elements, in what political context (in the widest sense, including church politics) the various groups and figures were operating, how the various competing doctrines were propagated, which ones were repressed (by whom and for what reason), which ones cultivated and fostered (by whom and for what reasons). It isn't exactly the case that "rationality" in some very general sense plays *no role whatever* in this story. In some parts it may well have acted in the background, but the idea that this is a story the essential movement of which is driven exclusively by a push toward (or against) the Enlightenment version of Reason, a story which can comprehensibly be reconstructed on those terms, seems entirely fanciful. Questions of absolute truth or Reason are at best subordinate in historical enquiry, and can be put aside there. This does not, or at any rate need not, imply, of course, that "there is no truth," only that our judgments about the truth or the rationality of various claims that need to be treated in the course of this historical enquiry are not of overwhelming relevance. Representatives of a dogmatic Enlightenment who attempt to ride their hobbyhorse of an abstractly construed "Reason" through the jungle of history either don't seem to get the point of the historical enterprise at all, or they show a character defect in their excessive readiness to refer everything to their own preoccupations.

If the ethos of Enlightenment really requires a self-critical investigation of our history and our historical knowledge, and one that is as free of prejudice as possible, then it seems right to try to develop some sensitivity to the kinds of questions the systematic pursuit of historical knowledge raises. The non-dogmatic partisan of Enlightenment would have to develop a "historical sense"; traditional philosophy will, as Nietzsche noted in the passage cited above, be of no use in this, unless one could transform it radically by "historicising" it. What, though, would it mean to undo and reverse the "de-historicisation" of philosophy? As a first approximation I suggest that "historicising thought" might be considered to have the following properties:

1. It recognises that the past was *different* from the present (at least in certain aspects that are of particular interest to us).
2. It assumes historical contingency: no laws of strict necessity determine the course of historical events.
3. It treats the past as relevant to the present.

One might think that the first of these three points is perfectly trivial. After all, even Homer could be said to be thinking in a "historicising" way when he mentions that heroes of an earlier generation were "different" from men now, at any rate significantly stronger than any of his contemporaries. Stones today are like stones yesterday, but the hero Diomedes was able to pick up easily with one hand a stone "which two men, as mortal men now are, would scarce be able to carry" (*Iliad* V. 302–305). One is thinking in a "historicising" way if one focuses on differences between the practice of democracy (and the concept of "democracy") in the ancient world and in twentieth- or twenty-first-century Europe, and tries to understand and to give some kind of general and theoretical account of these differences. Thus, "elections" (especially "multi-party elections"), considered to be a central characteristic of democratic regimes in the twentieth century, were vigorously rejected as "anti-democratic" in the ancient world because they gave an advantage to those who were wealthier, more eloquent, more knowledgeable, better known, or more personable, and the very existence of distinct "parties," even more of organised parties, would have been thought by the major ancient political thinkers to be a very bad sign indeed. It would be a form of "historicisation" to point out that what we retrospectively call "religion" in the ancient world was something completely different from "religion" in the post-Christian era: if one wants to speak of "ancient religion" at all, it was one without a scripture, without anything like a "church" structure, without "dogmas," "doctrines," or "creeds."

The second point refers to the way in which historicising approaches attempt to keep their distance from the absolutising of any form of necessity, whether it be mythical, metaphysical, logical, natural, or semantic necessity. The mere use of the conditional implies a knowledge that not everything happens "of necesssity."[8] To take my example again from the *Iliad*, at the beginning of Book II, Agamemnon puts the Greeks to the test by making a proposal to them which he does not wish or expect them to accept, namely that they abandon the siege of Troy and return home immediately. To his great surprise and disappointment, his proposal is greeted with loud approval, and the troops begin to prepare the ships for embarking. At this point Homer interrupts the narrative to remark: If no one had intervened, then the Greeks would have returned safely home, contrary to what fate had planned for them. Someone, however, does intervene: the goddess Hera, inveterate enemy of the Trojans, confers with Athena, explains the situation to her, and the two set about preventing the premature departure of the Greeks. Athena, in turn, has her favourite, Odysseus, act to stop the dissolution of the army. If Hera had not done that, Homer says, the Greeks would have got away, beyond and contrary to fate (*Iliad* II. 155). So there was in a certain sense a mythic necessity, which prescribed that the Greeks were to destroy Troy, but a deviation from this fated path was obviously not unthinkable for Hera, who can be assumed to know about these things, and who saw that she needed to act herself to put things back into order, that is, into the state she preferred, the eventual destruction of Troy by the Greeks.

Another and slightly more complex example can be found in Pindar's *Pythian 4*. Pindar tells how, on the return voyage from their quest of the golden fleece, the Argonauts landed on the island of Thera, and he reproduces (ll. 13–55) a prophecy made by Medea, who was with them. Like the seer Kolchas in the *Iliad* (I. 70), Medea knows "what was, what is and what shall be." She recounts how, before arriving at Thera, the Argonauts had crossed the African desert—she says they carried their ship for twelve long days (ll. 25–27). When they finally reached the coast and were about to raise anchor (ll. 24–25), a god appeared and offered one of them, a certain Euphamus, dominion over Libya (that is, Africa). Since, however, Euphamus was in a hurry to return home (ll. 32–33), he was not able to take over the exercise of this dominion immediately. So the hospitable god gave him a magic clump of African earth (l. 36) to serve as a pledge and guarantee of his lordship. Unfortunately, the magic clump of earth was swept overboard and lost in the sea voyage to Thera. One might think it in no way surprising that Medea knows all this: after all, she was there when it all happened and need do no more than exercise her memory, but she claims also to know what will happen in the future: a descendant of Euphamus will one day visit the oracle at Delphi, and he will get a commission from the god which he does not expect, and perhaps did not even want. He will be instructed to go and found a settlement in Libya. In doing so, he will take up his inheritance, the dominion over Libya which the god once promised him, or rather once promised one of his fore-fathers Pindar has already mentioned (l. 10) that Battus, the founder of the Libyan city of Cyrene, is a descendant of Euphamus "in the seventeenth generation." Archesilaus, the victor in the chariot race at Delphi to whom this Pindaric victory ode is dedicated, stands at the end of the genealogical series: he is a descendant of Battus (in the eighth generation).

What is most interesting about this passage, though, is that Medea not only predicts the future, but she reports about a possible future that will not be realised. She knows what *would have happened, if*. If the crew had paid attention, as she told them to, they would not have lost the divine clump of earth. If this had happened, Euphamus, when he eventually arrived home, would still have had the clump of earth and could have thrown it into the mouth of Hades near Taenarum. In that case, one of his descendants in the *fourth* generation would have conquered and settled Libya. This is, of course, a good example of a kind of colonialist ideology with which we have become familiar: God gave us this land for our own, so when we suddenly come over the horizon, conquer the place and murder, drive out, or enslave the inhabitants, this is really to be interpreted as our "return," because our ancestors, many generations ago (for instance, seventeen genera-tions ago) were here. The course which the actual story takes is con-tingent: only because the crew of the *Argo,* despite Medea's repeated warnings (ll. 40–41), happened to fail to pay sufficient attention, and Euphamus's magic clod was lost, but this need not have happened. Nevertheless, a certain mythic necessity does structure the narrative, because the end of the story, if not the details of the way in which that end is reached, is considered to be fixed. A gifted seer can know in general what will eventuate in the long run, but this knowledge will also be limited, because in the short and middle terms humans can act differently—one way or another—and what happens *in the short term* is dependent on that, on what they do and fail to do. Not even Medea could know antecedently whether or not the crew would be sufficiently careful—that is why she is so persistent in warning them. However, in the long run the deviations of human action from the prescribed, fated plan and the dark regions of ignorance in the visual field of the seer are insignificant, because the seer can be sure that the gods will make it their business to intervene in events again and again until the preferred outcome, for instance the rule of the descendants of Euphamus in Cyrene, has been brought about.[9]

Since "historicisation" is not an ontological, but an epistemic and methodological category, mythologizing and historicising approaches are not necessarily mutually exclusive. To see how this might be possible, consider a case like that of a bank which decides to sell all its assets of a certain type. In some very obvious sense this decision can be understood as one single ontological event (even if, for some purposes, it is construed as a temporally extended one). Nonetheless, one can look at it from a variety of different perspectives with a view to answering a wide variety of different questions. For instance: Why did the directors make this decision? Was it wise? Was it compatible with the existing laws regulating banks? Was it consistent with the general financial policy announced by the bank? Was this decision what set off the crash of the banking system which occurred shortly after it was made? These are all legitimate questions, but to answer them we need to use different methods. To find out whether the decision was legal, one would have, presumably to consult law books and judges. The judge who is qualified to give an opinion about the legality of the decision won't necessarily be able to say with any authority whether the course of action taken was wise or advantageous. Of course, in some cases there can be overlaps between different questions, and in the methods needed to answer them. Whether or not a certain decision is wise may depend in some cases on whether it is legal (and on the probability that an illegal act will be discovered and sanctioned). In a not completely dissimilar way, then, Medea can place contingent historical details—the crew was careless, the magic clump was swept overboard—in the larger framework of mythic necessity without necessarily destroying this framework. Logical and natural necessity replace in the modern world the mythic connections that played such an important role in antiquity (and the divine providence of the Dark Ages), but "historicising" accounts focus on the contingency of processes, and the openness of the outcome. So Plato's account of the cyclical succession of forms of constitution (*Politeia* Books VIII and IX) is not "historicising" in the appropriate sense, because the sequence itself is supposed to have a quasi-logical necessity. Similarly, the summaries of the views of past philosophers which one sometimes finds in the work of Aristotle are not in any way precursors of historicising modes of thought, because he thinks he knows where the succession of theories is headed and what its endpoint is (namely, the distinctions he makes and the theses he defends; he is, in a way, the first "Whig-historian"[10]). Thus the positions of earlier philosophers that are passed in review at the start of *Metaphysics*[11] are presented as if "philosophy" was a child that was passing through a series of transformations before reaching its mature and fully internally articulated form (which is assumed to be Aristotelianism). If this is the case, the "historical" parts of his writings have only pedagogical or antiquarian value or as a raree-show of striking zoological monsters. Anyone who had a strictly philosophically cognitive interest in metaphysical concepts like "cause" could simply start with Aristotle's own discussion of the "four causes" and spare the detour through past positions. Marx said of the bourgeois economists of the eighteenth and nineteenth centuries: for them, there *had been* history, but there was no history anymore;[12] the same was true of Aristotle.

This leads naturally to the third property: a historicising approach differs from most more traditional modes of thought in that it is concrete and tries to establish a relation of relevance between a past recognised as very different and the present.

In a world that is ambiguous and uncertain, as our world is, practical orientation depends in part on cognitive success: those who can see better have a better chance of finding nutritious material to eat, and thus better chances of survival; those who recall what happened the last time a member of the tribe ate the tempting but poisonous red berries on this bush will spare themselves at the very least an uncomfortable night. The accumulation of many observations is probably an important precondition for the rise of empirical science, but many traditional philosophical views claim that theories, once formulated, can be abstracted from the context of the accidental observations which lead to their formation. The very primitive theory "These red berries are not good to eat" is one I might form because I see what happens to my friends X, Y, and Z when they eat these berries, but if the theory is to be useful (or "valid" or "true") it must not depend on these specific observations. One can understand the theory without recourse to this specific chain of experiences, and one could have formed the same theory on the basis of completely different observations, because it is supposed to hold for all cases and thus be confirmed by any possible further observation. The so-called "positivists" of the early twentieth century spoke of a distinction between a context of discovery and a context of justification, and claimed that, no matter how one actually came originally to form the theory, when it comes to testing it, it must be completely detached from its origin.[13] Only when the theory is completely isolated and standing, as it were, on its own two feet alone, can one begin to establish its possible validity and value. What is important is not the particular past, the specific experiences and observation that led someone to formulate the theory, but the possibility at any given time of reconfirming it and the expectations to which it gives rise.

Usually the philosophical tradition was intent on pressing a second form of abstraction on us. It demands that a theory, in addition to being isolated from the context of its origin, must also be couched in

terms that are as temporally neutral, as "timeless," as possible, even
if these leave out important aspects of the subject under consideration.
Berries that are poisonous in Serbia are equally poisonous in Germany, that is, not suitable for consumption by anyone anywhere.
Aristotle is quite right to observe that fire burns in Persia as in
Greece,[14] but this is not obviously equally true for the sorts of "things"
historicising thought is concerned with, because human societies are
not natural phenomena. Clerics do not have the power to have you
turned over to the secular arm and burned at the stake in twenty-
first-century Britain that they had in certain parts of late-medieval
Italy. A human society carries its past along with it. We in Great
Britain have *this* form of government (the "Queen in Parliament") as
the final result (for the moment) of our specific history; people in
France have a different, historically equally conditioned system; the
Chinese have yet a different one. The past is not a closed book, which
can be investigated if one happens to have antiquarian interests, but
which otherwise has no relevance to us. Rather it marks our present
in a way which leaves us no choice but to engage with it. If we want
to orient ourselves theoretically and practically in this world—and
how would we avoid that even if we wished to try?—we must take
account of our past and relate our present to it.

Completely historicised sciences are in fact always constructed
around two sequences of pasts. First there are the series of observations made and the theories framed by past thinkers; second, there
is the sequence of past social formations within which these observations were made. Thus, the Pseudo-Xenophon (also called the "Old
Oligarch") thinks A, B, C, whereas Hobbes holds that D, E, F, and
Rousseau proposes G, H, I (first sequence). Pseudo-Xenophon was
(most likely) an internal analyst of fifth-century democratic Athens,
Hobbes was writing in absolutist France while observing the English Civil War, Commonwealth, and Restoration, and Rousseau
compared the republican institutions of Geneva with absolutist
France (second sequence). In epistemically favoured circumstances
we in the present can look back at past theorising and see both *what*

theorists of the past saw and also *from what standpoint* they were observing and judging what they saw. One of the things that we can clearly recognise in this is that past theorists were dependent on forms of experience which they had *within* the confines of past institutions and practices, and these are institutions and practices the limitations of which are now self-evident to us. This strongly suggests that we should try to apply this same insight to ourselves, our own experience and our purported forms of knowledge, and see if we cannot distance ourselves from effectively assuming that our own standpoint is absolute.

Neither the periodically recurring change of seasons, nor the logical succession of propositions in a geometric proof, nor the development of an infant into what we call a "grown-up" is a good model for historicising forms of knowledge. To put it paradoxically, (fully) historicised forms of thought can develop only in societies where there is no firmly rooted philosophy of history, no concept of fate, no divine providence, no natural teleology, and no overriding laws of development prescribed by reason or nature. That is, they can emerge only where socialised humans know that they are left to themselves and their own devices. This is one sense of "freedom."

Are "genealogies," then, good examples of "historical thinking" in the sense set out in the quotation from Nietzsche at the beginning? Yes, provided, of course, that one distinguishes proper genealogies from their pseudomorphs.

Before trying to say something about "genealogy," it is important to set aside some persistent misconceptions. One sometimes sees the term "genealogy" used as if this referred to a very specific method of enquiry—"the genealogical method"—as if it were something which was parallel to "the inductive method," "the deductive method," "the method of observation," and "the method of appeal to authority," that is, as if it were a specification of a series of steps that could be taken to confirm, validate, corroborate, or support some statement or theory (or to disconfirm, invalidate, and undermine it). The models employed to illustrate the application of one of these methods are, in the first instance, knowledge claims. "How do you know you are right to claim that there is a cat in the next room?" "Go in and look for yourself" (method of observation). "How do you know that most of the coins in your left pocket are 20p pieces?" "I have emptied my pocket and found it to contain seven coins: the first, second, fourth, fifth, sixth, and seventh investigated were visibly 20p pieces; the third was a 10p piece" (method of induction). Not all methods are infallible, or even highly reliable and, for that matter, not all methods are at all sound. Traditionally, philosophers have been especially hard on the "method of appeal to authority," and one can see why that might be. "Why do you think that homosexuality is an 'intrinsic evil?'" "Because the Pope (John Paul II, 1993) says so." On the other hand, it is beyond reasonable doubt that some appeals to authority are perfectly warranted. If I wake up on the operating table to answer the question "Why are you letting this man saw through your breastbone like this?" my answer (after the obvious "I was nicely narcotised, you fool, why have you woken me up") might be "The NHS consultant cardiologist told me I needed a bypass operation." This is perfectly pertinent and convincing. Of course, the consultant could be wrong, or I could have fallen for an elaborate hoax when I went to Papworth Medical Centre and I could there have spoken to someone who was not at all an NHS consultant cardiologist, but something else altogether. The details of such a situation I will not further elaborate, but those are all separate issues. Similarly, it is not unreasonable to believe that a certain piece of music I hear is in a certain key (rather than some other key) because Hilary, who has perfect pitch and a PhD in musicology, says so when she hears it. In fact, the more one thinks about it, the larger the swathe of opinions we have that we will find to be based on authority. Why do I believe that Warsaw is the capital of Poland, or that rabies can be caused by the bite of an infected animal, or that the planet Mars has two moons? Because I read it somewhere or someone told me. To be sure, if I have good specific reason, or am of an untrusting disposition, or if the context makes me suspicious, I can (sometimes) try to assess the reliability of the authority. Sometimes, this is easy. I take the notes of a piece of music and look at them to see the key signature, then I play the piece without showing Hilary the notes and observe that she always gives the correct answer. Testing the reliability of other witnesses (for instance, the Pope in matter of morals) may be much more complex.

Tests for reliability are generally not infallible either, nor can I even try to apply them to more than an infinitesimally small number of the "authorities" on which most of my beliefs rest. If it is thought that I am not "really" using "the method of appeal to authority" because I *could* in principle and if pressed, try to test the reliability of the authority, one would have to be ready to accept a similar kind of argument about induction, because in principle when I do my induction over the contents of my pocket, if you deny that the first piece is a 20p coin, I can try to use variants of the method of appeal to authority, for instance, asking other people to look at the coin and say that they think. Does this show that induction is based on authority?

"Genealogy," however, in any case, does not belong in *this* context of discussion at all. One should think of "genealogy" not as parallel to "induction," "appeal to authority," "deduction," and so forth, but as like "zoo-logy" (the study of animals), "geo-logy" (the study of the earth), "myco-logy" (the study of mushrooms), or "topo-logy" (the study of places and spaces). That is, it designates the area or domain of interest which is to be investigated. The domain of objects of "genealogy" is the "historical origins of things," especially where the "things" in question are the result of historically extended strands or sequences of successive acts of generation. So, to illustrate what is meant with a few obvious examples, in Book VI of the *Iliad* the Greek hero Diomedes encounters the Trojan Glaukus on the battle field and asks him who he is (ll. 119–236), and Glaukus gives his genealogy: "Aeolus begat Sisyphus who begat Glaukus [the First] who begat Bellerophon, who begat Hippolochus, who begat *me,* Glaukus [the Second]." The "genealogy" is the study of the successive strands of one human begetting another. Similarly, with ancient manuscripts that were reproduced by hand-copying before the invention of print, I can try to study the "origins" of some given text that I have before me, say Cicero's *de finibus*. The text I have was put together by a philologist who studied eight main manuscripts, one written in the eleventh century, three from the fourteenth century, two from the thirteenth century, and two from the fifteenth century. Obviously, Cicero did not compose the text in the eleventh century, so that manuscript must have been copied from earlier texts that were, probably, in their turn copied from earlier texts. "Genealogy" studies the historical sequence of acts of writing, each one of which generates a text, which may then itself be further copied. Finally, the Roman Catholic Church holds the doctrine of "apostolic succession," according to which, every recognized bishop in the Catholic Church is a direct successor of one of the original Apostles, and is thereby endowed with a certain number of spiritual powers and competences, which eventually derive from Jesus himself. Jesus, so the doctrine runs, is the absolute beginning and the legitimating source of all such powers. He possessed them in his own right, but decided to grant a certain number of them to his Apostles, and, through them, to their successors. The transmission of these powers takes place through a series of prescribed rituals and ceremonies, including an official "laying on of hands" in which an existing Apostle (or one of his successors, a bishop) publicly gives them over to someone who did not antecedently have them, but thereby becomes invested with them. So any given bishop in 2019 has those spiritual powers to the extent to which there is an unbroken historical line of transmission that connects him with one of the original twelve Apostles. This can be the object of "genealogy," that is, the study of the historical "origins" of the powers claimed by contemporary bishops, tracing back the sequence of historical steps by which these powers were purportedly transmitted sequentially from Jesus (ideally in unbroken succession) to Pope Francis.

Just as "biology," as the study of a certain domain, is not to be reduced to the employment of one particular "method," but rather develops and uses a variety of methods (observation, experimentation, idealisation, deductive reasoning, and so forth) depending on the particular research project in question, so similarly there is no reason to assume there is one specific "genealogical method," only one way to study the historical origins which form the objects of interest. A fortiori, pursuing "genealogical studies" need not be associated with a claim that the (nonexistent) singular "method" of genealogy in itself proves, supports, corroborates, disproves, or undermines anything whatever. I emphasise this point with such repulsive insistence because of the tendency some have shown to think that the whole project of "genealogy" can be quickly dismissed by appealing to "the genetic fallacy." The genetic fallacy is the mistake I would make if I used some fact about the origin of a statement to try to deny it was true (or, for that matter, prove that it was true). Those who like this terminology might say that I confuse the genesis or origin of the statement with its "validity." So, if Mr. X, who hates me and wishes me to fail, points out that I have made a mistake in some calculation I present, it would be an instance of the genetic fallacy for me to reject his criticism of my calculation on the grounds that it had its origin in his desire to discredit me. If the calculation is false—and we have clear, agreed-upon methods for determining this—then all that matters is whether the calculation does or does not give the right result. What Mr. X's motivations were in pointing out the mistake, is strictly irrelevant to the correctness of my calculation, although they may, of course, be perfectly relevant to some other enquiries made in other contexts. Thus, if I am a psychologist investigating how hatred focuses the attention, Mr. X's state of mind will most likely be relevant.

So just because the genetic fallacy *is* clearly a fallacy does not mean that "genealogy" is a disciplinary non-starter. If I am an ancient Lykian and Glaukus says to me: "Do as I say, *because* I am your king," then I am unlikely to try to deny or refute this claim by simply reciting his genealogy and stating that *because* he was begot by Hippolochus, he has no right to command me. He thinks he has a right to command me precisely because Hippolochus begat him. I can, of course, try to give an alternative genealogy, asserting that Glaukus is not the son of Hippolochus but the bastard offspring of a relation between Hittite slave and a local prostitute, but I would know that, or have discovered that, by the usual empirical methods—whatever methods were available for determining paternity. There would be no special "genealogical" method for discovering this. Of course, in the envisaged situation the whole discussion rests on the acceptance by both parties of the right of a king to command and the automatic acquisition of that right by, say, the eldest son of the ruling king, when that king dies. Another way I, as an ancient Lykian, could try to refute Glaukus's claim to be king would be to deny that there should be any kings at all, or that Lykians should be subject to a king or that kingship should be transmitted hereditarily. I might be able to argue for one or more of these claims, but if I did, I would not be using some special kind of "genealogical method" to do so. If I wanted to argue persuasively, I would be using whatever methods of political and sub-philosophical argumentation I could muster that would seem to me likely to be convincing. Anyone can commit the genetic fallacy anywhere. A particular kind of genealogy might be confused, pointless, flawed, irrational, fanciful, or vitiated by deep incoherencies of reasoning, but this will not be because "genealogies" in general *must* be congenitally committed to committing the genetic fallacy.

I would like to distinguish three kinds of "genealogical" research projects that have been developed to study historical origins systematically. By a "research project" I mean a kind of enquiry into a certain subject matter with particular questions in mind or with a particular purpose. So one kind of "biological research project" might be to study living organisms (biological entities) with the intention of making them as useful as possible to humans, who were assumed to have a certain set of needs and purposes; another might be to study living organisms in order to discover how relations of equilibrium between different species may be fostered in the interests of maintaining biodiversity; a third could be a study of the way biological organisms manage their boundaries with the external environment (something we could be interested in for a variety of reasons) or how they are affected by patterns of light and darkness, or how food chains get established in particular environments. These different programmes of study would presumably use a variety of different specific methods.

The three forms of genealogical research I want to distinguish are: first, "genealogy as study of primordial origination and founding (*Urstiftung*) in the interests of legitimation of some current practice," second, "genealogy as the study of convergences with the intention of showing that certain of our standard forms of conceptualisation and thought were virtually unavoidable when we emerged from the state of nature,"[15] and finally, "genealogy as dispersal of purported unitary origins and dissolution of meanings." Nietzsche rejected the first two forms and practiced the third.

The first type of genealogy is the study of a certain institution, practice, identity, or bundle of rights, powers, and claims to authority, with an eye to showing the legitimacy of the institution or practice in question. This type of project generally assumed that there was a single original source of meaning, validity, and authority in the past, and the investigation is devoted to trying to discover the relation in which this practice or institution stands to that aboriginal source of meaning and authority. So to return to the Roman Catholic doctrine of "apostolic succession," the high dignitaries in the Catholic Church are considered to have a set of powers, rights, and responsibilities which form a meaningful unitary whole and which depend on a single divine act of institution or inauguration which took place in Palestine during the time of the early Roman Empire. Jesus had all these powers and was the source of absolute legitimacy; he was the utterly singular point of origination of them. Each bishop today gets his legitimacy from the miracle-working *Wunderrabbi* of the first century who was crucified under Pontius Pilate, and the "genealogical study" tries to trace the transmission of episcopal power and legitimacy back explicitly in an unbroken line to that original foundation. Tracing the historical line does not *itself* give legitimacy, and finding a break in the chain or a deviancy does not undermine legitimacy *except in connection with the theological story* in which doing the genealogical research is embedded, and which gives it its focus. Thus, if I had a different theological story, for instance if I thought bishops derived their power from an obvious charisma which showed them to be bearers of divine grace, or if I thought they had what power they have because they were freely chosen by the members of their community, I could look at breaks and gaps in the genealogical succession with complete equanimity.

Nietzsche struggles against this first type of "genealogical thinking" because he considers it to be completely mendacious and utterly unhistorical. It is "unhistorical" because there are no absolute beginnings, origins, or initiations in history. Even Christian believers now admit that Christianity did not originate in a single "big bang" in the ancient Roman province of Judea, but was formed in a syncretistic process in which a great number of different elements collided, converged, coalesced, and were forced together over generations. Jesus did not invent monotheism, which was already in existence since the sixth century BC in Greece and Mesopotamia, and he had little interest in the Greek philosophical speculations that were to play such a great role in the genesis of what we call Christianity. Various conceptual items that seem to have been invented by Saul / Paul played an important role in the eventual Christian synthesis, as did elements taken from mystery religions, bits of Roman legal thinking, and so forth. The closer one looks, the more roots one discovers, and the more diverse these roots are, and the further back behind the purported "absolute origin" one can trace them.

The second reason for saying that this form of genealogy is "unhistorical" is that in this kind of account one generally finds that the historical transitions from one stage or phase to the next are presented in an overly simplified way, which forces them to conform to a schema that artificially imposes a pregiven meaning on them. However, the rituals that constituted the consecration of a bishop in second-century Spain were certainly not "the same" as those in use in Africa in the late twentieth century, nor were the associated ideas of those participating about what actually was happening.

So a genealogy of this first type starts from a purported single point in the past when Jesus transmits certain powers to his Apostles, and traces a further history of transmissions in an unbroken line down to the multiplicity of bishops who exist today. It is assumed that at the end of this process, that is, today, all these bishops have at their disposal a set of competences that are coherent and legitimate, and that form a kind of unity. There is a unity of meaning "episcopal power" that stands at the beginning and at the end of the process and is historically invariable.

The second type of genealogy tells the story of the exit from a "state of nature." It generally operates, although often not explicitly, with some concept of a convergence of the reasons operating in a variety of different circumstances which finally leads to the conclusion that certain outcomes are virtually inevitable, and in this way it gives some kind of justification. If, state of nature theorists argue, you understand certain almost universal features of the human condition, you can see that it is not merely an accident that we develop a certain practice which bundles together tightly a number of different elements. You may tell a kind of idealised historical story of how, through a succession of steps, it becomes clear how, under the circumstances, it was "natural," "sensible," "comprehensible," "almost inevitable" that these different elements came together to form the ostensible unity they did. Thus, in the early modern period, "sovereignty" was a key concept designating a bundle of different powers that states claimed for themselves. These powers included, for instance, the power to control borders and the power to coin money. They are, one might think, two different things, but the state of nature argument tries to show that it is perfectly reasonable for them to come together and be located in the *same* unitary structure, the "sovereign," and that this will be true in a wide variety of circumstances. This kind of genealogical thinking has some structural similarities with the prophetic wisdom of Medea, which was discussed earlier in this chapter. Medea knew that there was a fixed endpoint, the dominion of the descendants of Euphamus over Africa, which would eventuate, no matter what diverse historical paths human action and history took. So equally for "state-of-nature" genealogists there is an endpoint which is so highly privileged by its overwhelming rationality as a solution to some invariant problems that the difference in the starting point and huge variations in the actual development are largely irrelevant for understanding. This is true even if, in contrast to the case of Medea, no one at the beginning of the process knows, or can know what, at that time, the endpoint will be. Thus, some theorist might claim, the invention of the "hammer" was a unique and overwhelmingly optimal solution to a whole variety of problems with which all human societies are sooner or later confronted. If that is the case, then, sooner or later, something like a hammer will be invented (or imported), and the details of that process by which a particular society acquires hammers are less important for understanding "the hammer" than seeing why it is the uniquely suited instrument it is, and thus that its adoption is, sooner or later, virtually inevitable. Whatever the usefulness of modes of enquiry like this for understanding particular artefacts, like the hammer, this procedure will fail when it comes to giving an account of our basic apparatus of rationality and notions like those of "objectivity," if only because it will tend to become circular, explaining how we were (virtually) fated to acquire the concept we have *because* it can be shown to have emerged through a historical series of "rational" responses to situations. Certainly this mode of arguing is not a good instance of historical thought; it was never intended to be that, and in fact one might suspect that its attraction, like the attraction of many other forms of "state-of-nature" theory, is precisely that it seems to allow those who use it to avoid anything properly historical.

Nietzsche's third type of genealogy is structured in a way completely different from either of these two pseudomorphs.[16] It differs from the first pseudomorph in that it does not assume there is a past absolute origin for anything. It also differs radically from the second kind of genealogy in that it operates in exactly the opposite way to state of nature theories. State of nature arguments, even if they work by sketching a series of historical or quasi-historical steps that are to lead from "nature" to the emergence of whatever it is that is being explained, assume that at each step in the process the transition is natural, rational, reasonable, to be expected. Nietzsche, on the other hand, emphasises that the historical process is highly accidental (not "virtually inevitable") and that the elements that coalesce are not almost predestined natural partners but are *forced together*.

Nietzsche starts from an analysis of a contemporary situation, and notices that we take our world to be self-evidently structured around certain "unities," and these are construed as units of meaning. These "unities" could be things such as value systems (for instance, "Christian values"), institutions (the penal system), kinds of practices or disciplines (psychoanalysis), or "identities" (homosexual, frigid woman, masturbating child, delinquent). These "unities" present themselves to us as if they were constituted by elements that "belong together" and naturally cohere with each other. It is "no accident" that a bishop, who is a consecrated spiritual shepherd of his flock, preaches to its members, but also hears their confessions, presides over the ecclesiastical court, is responsible for diocesan finances, and represents the diocese in various public contexts. These things, these different functions, actually have had very varied historical origins and have very little to do with each other—why should a good preacher also be a good judge or a good financial administrator? They have come to be instantiated together in the office of bishop only through a highly complex and contingent historical process, or, perhaps better, a series of different processes. Nevertheless, for whatever reason, we have now arrived in a situation in which we endow them with a purportedly unitary meaning ("episcopal") and imagine them as "obviously" belonging together. In the first type of genealogy we imaginatively, but misleadingly, try to project that unity of meaning back onto some originary act of foundation. As if Jesus himself, or at any rate the Apostle Peter, must have been, or ideally ought to have been responsible for the finances of "the Church" in addition to being a preacher, a judge, a dispenser of good advice. A similar process of pseudo-unification takes place in the case of certain social identities. Thus, to take another example in the spirit of Foucault, one common stereotype has it that it is "no accident" that a man who loves other men, also has an "effeminate" character, likes to use makeup, and so forth. The seemingly self-evident way in which such properties are thought to "go naturally together" is also an illusion generated by social and historical processes that have forced distinct elements together into what looks like a synthesis.

Under the sharp light of this third kind of genealogy, clear study of the realities of the past, all of the above-cited purported "unities" dissolve and the idea that there is an inherently "meaningful" connection between the elements of which they are composed loses its plausibility. There was no single moment of founding of Christianity, there is no "criminal personality" rooted in natural laws of psychology, and history cannot be understood as merely a series of repeated gestures—of the *same* gestures repeated again and again—in which powers are transmitted down the generations. Crimes were different in the ancient world, different from those defined in the legal code of any modern society, as were those who committed them. "The criminal" is not the same everywhere—he or she is a construct and must, to be understood, be located in his or her historical and social context, and it is certainly not the case that people who commit crimes everywhere have the "same" motivations or the same personality type; a fortiori it is not the case that the elements of a purported "criminal personality" cohere together everywhere because they "naturally" belong together or universal reason decrees that they "must" coexist in conjunction. The conjunction of monotheism with a speculative doctrine of individual salvation and a church structure modelled on the administration of the Roman Empire was a contingent historical fact. Roles and identities (bishop, homosexual) need to be historicised if they are to be understood. To be sure, one can thrust one's head into the sand, ignore the rest of the world, and adopt a "definition" of "bishop," for instance, following contemporary Catholic canon law. It can make perfect sense, in particular, fixed, and well-defined contexts, to adopt this policy. If one is conducting a court case in an ecclesiastical court, there would perhaps be nothing amiss with proceeding in this way. However, what is, or should be, at issue here, is not to acquire a utilitarian guide to successful behaviour within the framework of a set of institutions that is assumed, for the moment, not to change, but to attain some kind of proper understanding of what, for instance, a bishop is. The fact that one cannot say once and for all what would count as such a proper understanding in all cases is not an objection. One can, of course, be sceptical, and the sceptical impulse is almost always healthy, but philosophy traditionally aspired so seeking something more than merely providing the ability to manoeuvre around in an artificially simplified environment. Of course, people can invent new concepts, if they wish, they can try to look for stricter and more plausible definitions of given or frequently used concepts, they might try to change the meaning of certain terms or modify the function of certain linguistic forms. No one will go to prison for this, as things now stand in Europe, nor will they even necessarily be assigned to an imagined celestial correctional institute or a virtual Coventry for this. Nevertheless, the main question is not the possibility of giving sharp definitions of concepts, but the cognitive usefulness of this project. Definitions tend to get you nowhere, if you are not operating within a fixed system, but in the radically open world of human praxis and real politics. Concepts like "Christianity," "democracy," "property," "punishment," "childhood," "war," and "economy," which are deeply entrenched in our world and give it structure, get their content through their social context and through the history which is in part the history of the institutions in which they are embedded. It is this social history that one must understand.

Historically accidental conjunctions, forced marriages of different elements, can, under some circumstances, secrete a false sense of the coherence of their elements, of general meaningfulness, and even of self-evidence around themselves. History and genealogy can help break open the carapace of mystification that surrounds important parts of our social world. This is not the same thing as "refutation." Genealogical analysis ("critique") does not imply a rejection of the office of bishop, only the destruction of an illusion that is associated with it, the illusion that it is self-evident that the office and identity of "bishop" exists, and that it encompasses a purportedly systematically interconnected and unitary collection of powers, tasks, responsibilities, rights, and functions. To be sure, the genealogy will most likely undermine certain attempts to legitimise this identity because it will show them to be without foundation. This does not mean that there might not be reasons to bundle together some of the other rights and functions that are in fact located in the office, although one would then probably be obliged to specify what these reasons might be.

Nietzschean genealogies take history seriously in a way that makes them difficult to integrate into the dogmatic structures of the Enlightenment. In any case, the dogmatic Enlightenment committed suicide at the latest in the early twenty-first century in the torture chambers of Guantanamo Bay and Abu Ghraib and secret CIA prisons of Poland, Romania, and Afghanistan. Whether the ethos of Enlightenment will suffer the same fate is unclear, if only because it is by no means sure how long humanity itself will survive, given the ecological catastrophe we have created.

4

Life Is a Game

αἰὼν παῖς ἐστι παίζων, πεσσεύων
(Heraclitus, Fragment 52)

No, it isn't. "Games" are amusing or entertaining; they are fun, giving active enjoyment; they are not serious; in many cases they have rules: they start and finish at a definite point, and have some kind of fixed standards for evaluating performance; often, although not always, there is one (or more) clear winner(s) and one (or more) loser(s); if the possibility of a draw is admitted, there are clear rules for when that result occurs.

Human life, however,

1. has not overall been very amusing or entertaining or much fun for most of the people who have lived on the planet;
2. is not un-serious; rather, it defines what the "seriousness" is, with which "a mere game" is contrasted;
3. doesn't actually have anything like a set of fixed rules for evaluating performance.

To be sure, one can see the power of the temptation to compare various individual aspects of human life, or indeed human life itself overall and as a whole, to a game. Many individual human activities are teleologically oriented and rule-governed. I pay the milkman every few months *so that* he continues to deliver the milk, and I do this by leaving £100 in an envelope rolled up in the neck of the empty milk bottle, which I know he will pick up every Monday, Wednesday, and Friday morning and replace with a new full bottle. I haven't actually seen the milkman since we originally set up this arrangement some twenty years ago—he leaves the milk in the very early morning when I am usually sleeping. Another individual, or several, may have taken over the milk route, but they and I know that they can exchange these bank notes with other people through a series of complicated rule-governed procedures. Whoever picks up my £100 knows they can eventually use it to acquire things they need or want or pay for services. It is partly as a result of the predictable stability of the socially enforced rules for exchange that this comfortable practice, which conveniently ensures my supply of milk, can continue. Games recommend themselves to many as a model for human action because of their explicitness, particularly their explicitness in the matter of rules. There are books that codify the rules of bridge or go or chess, specifying how the game starts, the possible sequences of events, what counts as a valid procedure, how the game ends, and, in cases like chess, croquet, bridge, or go, how score is kept and who has succeeded in winning and who has lost.[1] For games like chess there is an algebraic system of notation of moves, which gives an internal account of each game, while strictly avoiding any reference to what are taken to be irrelevant circumstances. The algebraic notation tells one, for instance, that on the first move one of the players moved a certain figure in a certain way (as specified by the rules of chess), but not what the temperature in the room at that time was, what kind of shoes each of the two players were wearing (if any), or how many people were watching the game apart from the two players (if any).

It would very much simplify things, that is, it would make *understanding* human life easier, if it were like this, and, no doubt, "game" is sometimes a useful hermeneutic metaphor. Thus, Clifford Geertz in a much-cited paper considers the whole of Balinese culture through the lens of one of its characteristic institutions, the cockfight.[2] Geertz calls the cockfight "deep play" rather than a "game," but this terminological difference should make no difference in this context. The cockfight is a game because it is a form of activity governed by clear rules including rules for starting and for timekeeping. Highly complicated forms of betting on the outcome are associated with or even considered to be an integral part of the fight. The various rules of the game are "written down in palm-leaf manuscripts" and overseen by an umpire, and they specify a clear end (one cock killing the other) and thus a clear way in which success can be distinguished from failure. The cockfight has two groups of participants: one is the owners, handlers, and audience, all of whom bet on the outcome; the other is the two birds, equipped with six-inch razor spurs, who fight to the death. It is a game, of course, only for the humans involved, not for the birds: the humans follow the rules, the birds just fly at each other; the humans find the fight entertaining, if serious (and, if Geertz is right, profoundly meaningful); the birds are not entertained: at the end one (or both) of them is usually dead. Geertz takes the cockfight to be a metaphor of Balinese culture in particular, but I have always thought that it could also be read as a metaphor of two-tiered societies like the ones we in the West inhabit, in which small groups of bankers, financiers, and investors provide the mass of the rest of us with spurs, egg us on ("Red pepper is stuffed down their beaks and up their anuses to give them spirit"), and bet on the outcome. Still, it is at best a metaphor because it is illuminating by virtue of concentrating our attention and inviting us to look for parallels; in fact, human life in general and as a whole is not really much like a game of any kind at all. Just to repeat: first, for a game the question of how to individuate the action to be evaluated, and in particular how to determine what the appropriate goal is, relative to which it is to be evaluated, has a clear solution. This is not the case for human life. Second, which (that is, whose) standards of success and failure apply is usually given "internally" by the rules of a game, but in human life that is an open question.

One cock kills the other, or is itself killed, or both are killed, or one or both refuse to fight. Each person who bets on a cock has a clear goal: that that cock win. The go players place their stones in turn on one or another of the specified (as yet unoccupied) points of the board; the one who at the end has enclosed the largest amount of space (calculated by very strict rules) wins. But how is one to cut up into specified "actions" (or "moves") the whole sequence of actions which Churchill took during World War II as he tried to defeat Nazi Germany and thereby to preserve the global dominance of the Empire? As various external observers at the time saw very clearly, the means which Churchill adopted to attain his first goal (the defeat of Hitler), made it much more likely that he would fail to attain his ultimate goal (the survival of the Empire). It did not require much foresight to see that a Britain completely exhausted by total war and in alliance with two other larger powers, the USSR and the United States, *both* of which (for completely different reasons) were actively hostile to the continued existence of the Empire, would be unable to keep control of its enormous colonial possessions in Africa, Asia, and Oceania. Churchill knew very clearly that Stalin was no friend of the Empire, although he might be a useful ally against Hitler, but perhaps at the beginning he did not completely realise that fully two-thirds of German losses in military casualties and materiel would be on the Eastern Front and hence that this alliance would turn out to be as crucial as it was. However, not being by any means dull-witted, he must also at some level have known that the United States, too, was looking forward eagerly to the dissolution of the Empire, so that it could pounce on the resulting fragments and integrate them into an economic system under its own control. How did Churchill deal with this uncomfortable fact about his other great ally? Not being a historian, I don't know the answer to this question. I suspect his method of coping was a usual combination of means: focusing on the *immediate* task at hand (defeating the Third Reich), distracting himself and his attention, not thinking about things too carefully or clearly, compartmentalisation, and mystification (of self and of others). One can see the invention of the "special relationship" with the United States as a massive instance of such mystification. Human life in general is much more like this (very) brief account of Churchill in World War II than like the activities of a chess player, reported in algebraic notation as the official record of a match. It is characterised by a plurality of interlocking and also sometimes not fully articulated goals, and it proceeds following sometimes some fixed rules, but more often changing policies and guided by shifting and unclear general orienting principles.

People sometimes do have individual detached goals that seem to have no clear connection with the rest of their motivational set, although if the idiosyncracy and isolation become too extreme, we may enter the realm of pathology (fetishism). Thus, a recent survey of members of the Conservative Party in the United Kingdom found that a majority of them wanted a "no-deal" Brexit even if it was bad economically for the country as a whole, destroyed the Conservative Party as a political force, and broke up the Union by driving Scotland to secede. So "Brexit" seems to have become a singularity, a quasi-religious goal detached from the rest of politics, and, more importantly, detached even from the other traditional political concerns of the Conservative Party. However, it is also the case that the appearance of complete detachment that is exhibited by fetishes, religious manias, and phenomena like Brexit, usually disappears as one acquires more information about the people who are subject to these pathologies. Even if we are unwilling to say that the foot fetishist has "reasons" or "good grounds" for his obsession, at least, the more we learn about his history and behaviour, the more we will be able to locate his special concern in a wider context of perhaps unconscious desires, fantasies, and motivations, so that it will become less of an absolute singularity.

For most humans, our goals are generally not detached and atomistic, but nested. Most frequently we have sequentially nested sets of goals. I want to turn on the light, so that I can find my glasses, so that I can read, so that I can finish the book I am reading, so that I can write my report on it, and so on, and so on. In fact, the sequence of my goals may go on and on into the indefinite future before petering out, just by virtue of a failure of my imagination and knowledge and by sheer fatigue.

All of the above is by way of arguing for the non-applicability of the model of a game to human life as a whole. If player A moved a knight by the rules of chess, A has moved a knight, and this is true, *regardless* of the larger strategy within which the move is located. The move is defined by the rules of chess. On the other hand, in the case of Churchill, adopting a shorter-term framework (defeating Hitler in Europe) or longer-term framework (maintenance of the Empire) will cause one to give a different specification of what action is being performed and for what teleological end, and that can change the evaluation of success or failure of the action, *even if the same criteria of success and failure are used.* When Churchill, during the height of the invasion scare, sent a large number of tanks to Egypt, this was neither a clearly demented aberration nor a simple mistake: it was part of the "Defend the Empire" action even if it didn't really make a lot of sense as a contribution to defeating Hitler in Europe. In this case, the individuation of the act performed depends on the framework chosen, but both frameworks were ones Churchill himself could have used (and presumably did use), and the relevant time frame was his lifetime. However, it is perfectly open to us to use time scales that reach beyond an individual's lifetime. The ancients recognised this when they discussed "the fate of Priam," a happy and prosperous king whose city was destroyed just after his own death.[3] Should the fact that since the 1960s the Federal Republic of Germany has been significantly more prosperous than the rump-UK (shorn of the Empire) cause one to change one's evaluation of Churchill's action during the war? Did it merely *look* like a success in 1945, but do we now see that it was *actually* a failure? Human life is perhaps more like war than like chess, but in fact even war is too close to a game to be a very good model of life. After all, in war there are rules, specified detached actions (invasion, retreat, truce, and so forth), and some sense of closure through success or failure: if many of your main cities are razed to the ground by firebombing, including with atomic bombs, your

Emperor signs a capitulation, and your territory is occupied by your opponent's military without resistance, then you have "failed to win" the war, even if small groups of soldiers or individuals hold out for longer in isolated places, in one case until the 1970s.[4]

To say that mostly my goals are nested in clusters, systems, or sequences, rather than existing as free-standing individual aims, and thus that my life is subject to constant reevaluation even after my own death in the light of further events that occur is not to say that all my goals or desires necessarily cohere into one single system or network. I may wish to go to French lessons, so that I can improve my French, so that, in turn, I can express myself more clearly, converse more easily with my friends, and so forth. I may also try to repair Tabitha's cat flap, so that she can enter and exit the house more easily, but is protected from marauding intruder-cats, with the result that she becomes less stressed. There may be no obvious connection between my ability to speak more fluently to my friends in French and Tabitha's more relaxed state; they may simply be *two* distinct goals I have. To say that they "*must*" both form part of a single teleological network, because they are both goals I pursue, even though I am not aware of any such network or system, is just to try to impose on me a philosophical conception of a "unity" that has no phenomenal basis. Perhaps there is a single final causal or even neural unity, but that is surely a separate issue. Philosophers who are devoted to the unity of an individual human's projects often shift their ground from making a speculative metaphysical claim about unity grounded in human nature to exhortation: it isn't that, try as I might to avoid it, I *always of necessity* have a single final set of unified projects, but at any rate I "*ought*" to be trying to impose this particular construction on my life, that of seeing my goals as a (potentially) *unitary* totality. Perhaps they are right, and the exhortation is sensible, although I don't think so, but even if they are right, "you ought to impose a single goal on your desiring and acting" is not the same thing as "your desiring and acting (really) has a single goal (whether you know it or not)." What would be wrong with failing to impose unity? It might be inconvenient, even highly inconvenient, but surely whether or not it was would depend on a very large number of other factors that would have to be taken into account. Do we know a priori that in *all* cases the overall result on reflection would be that the convenience of unity outweighed the inconvenience of what I needed to do to impose such unity?

Not only, however, is the identification and individuation of action in real human life more difficult than in games; there may be a wide variety of different ways in which "failure" or "success" is evaluated or the criteria may just be unclear. Even in the case of games, where there are embedded institutional standards, and rules for scoring laid down in books, the individuals who engage in them may be pursuing their own goals and may perfectly appropriately evaluate the activity relative to those goals. If I am playing football for my health, I may reasonably count this activity as a failure if it results in constant broken bones, even if my team scores more than its opponents. It may even turn out that *everyone* on the football team is playing for reasons of health and has no genuine interest in the final score.

It is, of course, true that games can have grey areas in which it is not clear whether certain things are permitted or prohibited, and where there is a certain amount of disagreement about what the rules really are. Anyone who ever played as a child with children from a *different* neighbourhood or milieu knows that such variants in well-known games exist and give a certain kind of particularly obnoxious child their first outing as a litigator—the existence of such grey areas in informal play is one of the reasons that bodies like the Chess Association and the various organisations governing and regulating sports were originally founded. It is also true that games can in one sense remain identifiably the same while changing their rules. This is especially the case where there is such an overarching regulatory body, although here one can wonder whether it does not then become the tail wagging the dog. Nevertheless, if the rules are changing constantly and unpredictably—or even if one knows that they *could* change at any moment without warning—and if there is constant irreconcilable disagreement about what, in any case, the rules actually are—or, for that matter, whether there are any rules at all—as is the case with the living of a human life, then it is not at all clear what is gained by saying that what one has here is a case of a "game." That I (or anyone else) can arbitrarily decide to construe my life (or anyone's life) as (if it were) a game, is, of course, no more excluded as a logical possibility nor ethically prohibited than that I (or anyone else) can "construe" the slow sliding of two beads of water down a windowpane as a "race" between them, but then, construing it as a "race" has no *more* standing in telling me anything substantial about the water droplets themselves, than construing them as a set of binocular magnifying glasses, fit to improve the vision of an animal sitting on one side of the windowpane who wished to look at something on the other side, or as two children of Poseidon, antiphonically singing his praises, or as twin sublunary comets, the nipples of the goddess Thetis, tears from the weeping eyes of Niobe, or the window's homage to any two overweight twins.

It has often been pointed out that it is perfectly common, and considered perfectly acceptable, to contradict oneself palpably in what are called "proverbial" contexts: "A bird in the hand is worth two in the bush"; "All good things come to those who wait"; "Life is real, life is earnest / life is a dream"; "Life is a long, hard slog"; "Life is brief and fleeting." This seems to be because "proverbs" are taken to be statements that formulate in a pithy way certain *aspects* of life, and that a proverb aptly catches something about that aspect in no way implies that it exhausts *all* that can rightly be said. That is, there may be—in fact there is certain to be—more than one aspect to the phenomenon in question, and different proverbs formulate in a vivid way different things that are true about the phenomenon. To say (seriously) and in a non-proverbial context that life is a game is thus to make two mistakes. To take what is at best a metaphor to be reality ("the rules of life"); to take a metaphor that is *useful* in some limited contexts, and, abstracting it from that limited context, apply it, purportedly non-contextually, to a whole, the whole of human life. Or is philosophy itself best construed as a form of proverb spinning?

5

The Metaphysical Need and
the Utopian Impulse

Philosophers, and others, have in the past discussed a number of different ways in which the imagination impinges on different aspects of our life, such as the imaginative supplementation of what is in some sense immediately given to us in everyday perception so that we "see" three-dimensional objects and not two-dimensional patterns, the role of imaginary reconfigurations of important social institutions—for instance, the way in which we are trained to see our specific form of the market economy as especially "free"—and finally the large-scale forms of speculation, of the kind embodied in religions and large-scale social and political movements. So we have learned from Benedict Anderson's *Imagined Communities* that nationalism requires Muslim Javanese and animist Sumatrans to imagine themselves as "Indonesians," while presumably also imagining the Dutch administrators in Jakarta to be "not Indonesians," or the Catholic Bohemian resident of Prague to see the Protestant Moravians in a small village as "fellow-Czechs," but not his German-speaking neighbours in his own city.[1]

This chapter is a discussion of a set of connected topics involving such large-scale forms of speculation, which were very widely canvassed in the nineteenth and the first third of the twentieth centuries, but which have fallen rather out of fashion during the past fifty years or so in the sense that they are not even much discussed any more. These nineteenth-century views are centred around theses about certain ways in which humans are enticed to go beyond the world as we see it, our everyday universe and its familiar structures, and either imagine something "beyond" or even act to realise the content of an imaginary image of that which is radically different.

It seems to be a reasonably well supported hypothesis that all human societies give themselves some kind of general account about the world as a whole and their place in it. Let us at any rate assume that this is the case for the moment. These accounts can take a variety of different forms including myths, narratives, religious dogmas, philosophical theories, or world views. Religious and philosophical world views will be my main examples.

These general ways of looking at the world seem to have some striking properties. First, they seem to be non-utilitarian, a form of luxury; they go beyond what one would need to know for any obvious pragmatic purpose. They often provide some special concepts which give the mundane affairs of our world a kind of extra or surplus meaning: "This is not a decision to live together and support each other, but the Sacrament of Marriage" or "This is not a civil disturbance, but Revolution" or "This is not picking one deodorant rather than another or one set of almost indistinguishable politicians to rule us rather than another, but 'Autonomy' or 'Democracy.'"[2] Such concepts often show themselves particularly resistant to nominalist interpretation. Second, they seem to have deep practical effects on the way people act. Not only will martyrs allow themselves to be tortured and killed for what seem to outsiders to be utterly obscure and insignificant points of doctrine, but as the various wars of religion showed, they will also kill large numbers of people because those people refuse to accept a particular imaginative image of the world, and insist on remaining Protestant, rather than Catholic, or vice versa. Third, some of them are very persistent, even in the face of apparent refutation, so that one suspects that they are held for reasons that are not strictly cognitive.

At the beginning of the nineteenth century one could have found two different ways of thinking about how it came about that humans held these general accounts of their world, or, as the ancients put it, how humans began to philosophise. First, there was a very old view which was formulated clearly by Aristotle, who was essentially an extroverted biologist and natural historian rather on the model of David Attenborough, but who also engaged in a bit of general theorising on the side. Aristotle begins his *Metaphysics* with the assertion that all humans "by nature" desire to know. That is, we all have a deep-seated curiosity about the world around us and this causes us to want to see in a perspicuous way how the world is and understand why it is the way it is. Since the desire to know is naturally boundless, satisfaction can come only from some kind of complete view of everything. Given Aristotle's view about the connection between satisfying one's natural desires and experiencing pleasure, one can expect the satisfaction of our curiosity about the world to be associated with distinct pleasure.

This is very definitely not any kind of pragmatist view; that is, Aristotle does not hold that we desire to know what we need to know in order to make our way around in the world. He is very clear that the kind of speculation he is interested in comes to its fullest fruition when people have the luxury of leisure time, that is when they are precisely *not* trying to satisfy their basic biological needs in the most efficient way. This account of the origin and nature of world views does not, however, help us to understand one of the phenomenally most striking features of many of the historically most influential world views, which was mentioned above, namely their sometimes uncanny persistence. If we had a natural curiosity, and that was the end or at any rate the main burden of the story, why should we not be keen to find out something *new,* to come to a *better* understanding and thus to *change* our view of the world? So the keenest pleasure might then be in enquiring or even in finding out one had been wrong and acquiring a more adequate view than the one one had held. Philosophers in the ancient world were continually coming up with new systems, just as the ancient gods were constantly presented anew in unfamiliar combinations and under different aspects by ancient poets. For Christians in the Middle Ages, after all, curiosity was a vice precisely because it was thought to have this property of making people eager to move on to new views and lacking in loyalty to positions they had once taken.[3]

There was, however, at the start of the nineteenth century another way of thinking about world views which did not refer their origin in the first instance to the intellectual exuberance of human beings who had natural curiosity and leisure, but gave them a rather darker aetiology. This second strand emphasises the overwhelming experience of weakness, failure, pain, loss, disharmony in human life, and the difficulty we humans have in facing up to this fact and dealing with it in one way or another. If the more optimistic notions about the importance of our natural desire to know and a relaxed attitude toward its consequences is characteristic of the mainstream of ancient philosophy, this second strand is more closely associated with various religious views. One might think here of the Book of Job which is about apparently meaningless suffering, human weakness, and the pointlessness of human curiosity—as God helpfully points out to Job, he is not up to the task of understanding the foundations of the earth anyway, so what, one might reasonably ask, is the point of trying? This religious motif has a slightly subterranean life in the West, running with full force through St. Augustine. In his *Confessions* (Bk. XI, 12) Augustine considers the question of what God was doing before he created the world, and he canvasses the answer, apparently held by at least some Christians at the time, that he was preparing hell as a place of eternal torment for people who asked this kind of question. In the early nineteenth century this strand of thought emerges in a rather significantly modified form in some philosophical writers. Hegel, characteristically enough, has versions of *both* of the two strands of thought. On the one hand, in the main body of his work he has a story of the generation of the three great cultural artefacts—art, religion, and philosophy—as the teleological culmination of the development of (the human) spirit, which is essentially constituted by a desire to know. To be sure, Hegel thinks that this desire to know takes what one might think is the slightly peculiar form of a desire to know *itself*, that is, to understand and grasp itself "in concepts"—"Seinen Begriff zu erkennen gehört zur Natur des Geistes"[4]—but, given that everything that is is (in a sense to be specified by philosophy) "spirit," the injunction spirit gives itself to "know oneself" is not really a limitation on the universal desire to know. On the other hand, in some early writings Hegel has very strong traces of the other strand. Thus, he writes that "the need for philosophy" arises under highly specific social and historical circumstances, namely when "life has lost its 'unity.'"[5] Philosophy, then, is the attempt to replace the social and other bonds that have been lost or destroyed through speculation. We might think of this as an appeal to "the imagination" (although Hegel would not put it this way) in some uncertain relation to more strictly cognitive human faculties. One can easily see how prima facie implausible it is to think that such unity, if it ever in fact existed in human societies and was lost, could be reestablished by speculation alone. This, of course, was a line of argument Marx developed extensively. In fairness to Hegel, however, he did not think that abstract theorisation *alone* could solve what were actually social problems, but rather had a very complex theory about the way in which modern society had various real hidden resources, which were adequate to restore social unity and harmony if they were correctly understood, laid bare, and mobilised. The role of philosophy was imaginatively to activate them.

Still, two aspects of Hegel's claim are significant. First of all, it is highly significant that Hegel speaks of a "need" for philosophy rather than merely a desire or wish or interest. Human beings have all sorts of desires, wishes, and preferences, many of which are transitory, unimportant, or even whimsical. Even if Aristotle's "desire to know" is universal in all humans, that fact by itself does not yet tell us anything about how systemic this desire is or how urgent or important its satisfaction should be. Perhaps all humans occasionally desire to sneeze, but no one thinks that is important. Perhaps a desire always to think well of oneself and put one's own action in the best possible light is also universal, but we think this is rather a desire it would be good for us to resist and combat, or at least to try to control. When we speak of "desire" in cases like this we are usually adopting a first-person or intentional point of view of the subject. At least in pre-Freudian life I know what my desires are, and even in post-Freudian life "desires" will be attributed to me only when my own intentional action exhibits a certain subject-structured form. On the other hand, we sometimes use "interest" in a subjective way and sometimes in a more objective way. In either case, to speak of an "interest" is to speak of something which one "ought" to cultivate or continue to cultivate in a coherent or consistent way. To speak of an interest is roughly to speak of what it *would be rational* for me to desire to concern myself with—in a sufficiently flexible and open-ended sense of "rational"— even if we all know that I do not in fact always want what it would be rational for me to want. So you can say of me that I actually have an interest in preserving my health, even if I do not acknowledge it, because I "ought"—in some relatively abstract and objective sense of "ought"—to take care of my health, even if I do not at the moment want to, but I can also say that I have an interest in Greek poetry because I have not merely a momentary whim to read it, but have a coherent, long-term view that it is in some way objectively important to cultivate it, or that it will continue to be a source of enlightenment and pleasure for me, and I generally also have a desire to act on that view in appropriate circumstances.

A "need" is something of an entirely different character altogether from either a desire or an interest. A "need" is a conditio sine qua non of successful functioning, and as such has nothing in principle whatever to do with anything anyone might be aware of. So if I "need" a certain minimal caloric intake, that means that without that intake I will malfunction, and this is an objective state of affairs that has nothing in principle to do with what I might want or desire. To say I will "malfunction" does not necessarily mean I will die off immediately. I can live for months on a seriously inadequate diet, but it does mean that there will be distinct pathologies I will develop, perhaps diseases like scurvy or anemia. If I do have a need of which I am unaware, I can also say I have an interest in satisfying that need (even though I do not know that I have that interest). However, even if I am using "interest" in a strictly objective way, as when I say that you have an interest in maintaining a healthy non-privatised postal system, *even if you don't know it,* I am at most saying that you should wish to support such a system because it is really to your rational advantage, whether you recognise that or not. However, I can probably continue to function without pursuing or attaining everything that it would be to my rational advantage to pursue or attain. You might not eventually *like* a world without a public postal service, but I am not necessarily saying that you will seriously malfunction without it, in the way in which you will malfunction if one of your strict needs is not met.

The difficulty arises when one extends this analysis of "need" to the psychological and social domains. It seems rather clear, though, that there is no insuperable obstacle to forming psychological and social analogues to the concept of (physical or biological) malfunction, and that is sufficient to permit the range of the concept "need" to be appropriately extended.

This account would, I think, go some way toward explaining the persistence with which populations cling to their traditional religious beliefs. If those beliefs really did satisfy a need, even a psychological need for continuity—provided one can genuinely understand an interest in continuity of life as a *need*—then it is understandable that people will not give these beliefs up until and unless they either find a substitute which is shown to be equally good, a hard proposition when what is at issue is a complex structure which has lasted thousands of years, has constructed cathedrals, inspired paintings, and run large numbers of educational and charitable institutions. One further possibility, of course, would be not to satisfy the need in some other way, but to get rid of it altogether. The question would be whether that is possible at all, and, if so, how that might be possible. One of Hegel's predecessors, Kant, leads the way here in talking about reason and its needs, but he construed these needs as cognitive and atemporal. He had a complex theory of the nature of the human mind which had as one of its corollaries that the human cognitive apparatus really *could not function* without generating large-scale imaginative constructs like the "ideas" of the world as a whole, the soul, and God, and in that sense they satisfied a "need" we had and could claim a kind of legitimacy although they had no cognitive content. Oddly enough, then, Kant thought that things like metaphysical and religious world views were inescapable and essential for the functioning of the mind, but also had no truth value in the sense in which normal statements about the world, such as "Margot lives in Marburg" had truth value. He devoted much energy to examining various systematic ways in which the natural tendency of the mind to totalise might also result in *illegitimate* constructions. We see, he thought, that every event we encounter in the world has a cause and we then might be tempted to think that the world as a whole is a single huge event of which there is one cause. There is, as it were, one cause which is the cause of everything. This, Kant thinks, is the origin of the idea of God. This idea has some practical uses in that it gives us a useful practical directive, namely "whenever you find the cause of something, never stop there, because in principle that cause itself has a cause and you could go on indefinitely." To that extent it has a kind of legitimacy or a practical warrant. Nevertheless, this idea has no cognitive content of the kind Christian theology attributes to it. The same is true of the ideas of the soul to the extent to which this is more than a merely formal category. These were, as it were, necessary by-products or signs of the healthy functioning of our mind, "subjectively" necessary, he says, but also objectively contentless, and potentially very dangerous, because they could be incorrectly taken to be forms of cognition although they were not.[6]

This Kantian theory of a human need to which large speculative structures were a response construes this human need as essentially timeless, and his view is essentially individualist. The need is connected with the requirements of healthy functioning on the part of the human cognitive apparatus of each human individual, and that is assumed to be the same everywhere and at all times. Hegel's view is distinct from this in two aspects: first of all, Hegel does not share either Kant's individualism or the so-called faculty psychology to which Kant subscribed. "Faculty psychology" is an eighteenth-century invention, a programme which divides the human person up into distinct functional systems that do not have much to do with each other. For Hegel the need to which speculation is a response is not a mere feature of the isolated cognitive apparatus of each human being, but is a holistic property of human individuals (and groups): we need to see and understand ourselves as part of a group with which we can positively identify, and which collectively has a cognitive grip on the world as whole. This is as much an emotional and moral need as a cognitive one, and it is a need for which there could be only a collective form of satisfaction. Second, Hegel does not share Kant's exclusively atemporal orientation to the human world. For Hegel our needs, too, have their history.

That brings us to the second significant aspect of Hegel's claim that the need for philosophy arises when life has lost its unity: the context very strongly suggests that there was a time when life *had* its own unity, and philosophy would not only have been a luxury but would also have been so superfluous that it would not have existed at all as a serious enterprise. This idea that life had lost a unity which it had previously had, that there was something problematic or deficient or defective in their own society and the modern age in general which prevented their contemporaries from leading a full and happy life, was very widespread during the late eighteenth and early nineteenth centuries, and there was very wide agreement that what was wrong had something to do with a loss of forms of large-scale social identification or the fragmentation of human life. This disharmony or alienation was thought to have a number of interlinked aspects: (a) individuals experienced themselves as internally split rather than psychologically unified and felt unable to develop all their powers harmoniously, with the result that they became "one-sided" or felt mutilated; (b) being subject to particular sets of systematically and irreconcilably conflicting demands all of which had a hold and claim on the individual; (c) human populations saw themselves as divided into inherently antagonistically related groups; (d) individuals were unable to "identify with" and have a positive and affirmative attitude toward themselves, their fellow humans, and their social and political institutions; (e) human life in modern societies lacked "meaning."[7] This was also virtually universally construed as a *specifically contemporary* problem, that is, one specific to the late eighteenth and early nineteenth century. It was *not* thought to have beset the ancient Greeks (Schiller, Hölderlin, Hegel), the members of the Universal Church in the Middle Ages (Novalis), or immediate producers in precapitalist societies (Marx). If "ethics" is the discipline which helps us to understand what features of our world and life are difficult, dangerous, or problematic, and suggests ways of dealing with these features, this account makes it seem natural to try to supplement traditional forms of ethics with a philosophy of history.

I would like to point to the implausibility of the *comparative* claim that the ancient world exhibited "natural or unreflective or naive unity" of interests. Anyone who reads the history of Thucydides will find it hard to believe that each city was a beautifully structured harmonious concert of citizens with as yet undifferentiated interests.[8] Again, in fairness to Hegel, he is very clear that this view about a primordial state of unity is a kind of ideal type constructed for analytic purposes, a bit like the idea of a perfectly frictionless plane, and so it need not, and was not, ever actually instantiated, but still has value by virtue of throwing cognitive light on an important aspect of our situation.

I spoke above of several interlinked aspects of contemporary society to which the thinkers I am discussing took exception. Obviously these aspects can be seen to be connected if one takes as a tacit ideal the idea that a meaningful human life to be one in which psychologically unified individuals are able fully to develop their powers in a unified society with which they are able positively to identify and which imposes on them only coherent demands. The lack of a unitary world view which allowed me to identify with my world and society would then result in some distinctly pathological forms of human behaviour.

If there was a time, however, when life had its own unity, before the need for philosophy arose, then there might in principle be a time in which that unity was reconstituted as it were from within society itself. This raises the distinctly un-Kantian possibility which fascinated several later philosophers in the Hegelian tradition, among them Marx,[9] namely the idea that in a satisfactory society, from which certain kinds of deep-seated conflicts were absent, philosophy (along with religion) would be superfluous and would disappear. Of course, even in such a basically harmonious society there might be a pale successor-discipline to the antique magnificence of "philosophy," which might, for example, take the form of straightforward attempts to get an overview of the state of our knowledge or even suggestions for minor improvements in our social arrangements. People in such a society might have a use for a kind of encyclopedic summary of their knowledge, but they would not need anything like a traditional world view. *They* could be happy nominalists, living lives without dark shadows, "metaphysics," and deep, hidden meanings. One line of criticism of what are sometimes called "positivist" strands in twentieth-century philosophy consists in claiming that positivists in fact propound methods of direct observation and theory construction which would in principle be cognitively perfectly appropriate in a fundamentally harmonious society; however, by advocating the exclusive use of such methods in repressive and conflict-ridden societies like ours, they tacitly contribute to diverting attention from fundamental social antagonisms.[10]

One of Hegel's followers who took the possibility of a society without large-scale speculation seriously was Feuerbach,[11] although he was primarily concerned with theology rather than philosophy. He brought out in an especially vivid way something that Hegel and Kant had only gestured toward, namely that beneath various other rather superficial desires and interests humans have a vital need for self-affirmation which they will go to any lengths to satisfy. Despite themselves, Kant and Hegel were still in thrall to the traditional philosophical view that gave to cognition and the striving for propositional truth a central role in human life. To some extent Feuerbach ignores this and shifts the focus from the cognitive correctness of world views to the role speculative constructs play in our psychic economy; he concentrates on what we would probably call psychology, what he called "anthropology." For Feuerbach we were creatures of emotion and need, especially the needs we have for other people, rather than, even, potentially pure knowers. "Religion," he thought, arises out of human experience of weakness and failure, that is, experience of the direct negation of such self-affirmation. When we experience our weakness in some crucial area of endeavour, we genuinely find it difficult to face this fact directly, and so we attempt to compensate for it in imagination by creating the idea of a "Being" (God) who has exactly the powers we experience ourselves as lacking. This compensatory projection gives us a certain pseudo-sense of power, self-affirmation, and meaningfulness, a sense mediated through the imaginary Being. So the idea is that, for instance, the members of some extremely primitive tribes wish desperately to cross a river, and find that they cannot. They find it difficult if not impossible simply to accept this state of powerlessness, so compensate or console themselves with the imaginary thought of an entity to whom they are related and who can, or could, do exactly what they cannot. They can't cross the river, but they are the children of a God who could, if he wished. A consequence of this, Feuerbach thought, is that the more human powers develop, the more this imaginative projection becomes unnecessary. As its basis in experienced impotence progressively dissolves, the conception of "God" becomes ever thinner. When human powers are fully developed, we will be able to dispense with the compensatory fantasy altogether; thus, this theology loses its object. Feuerbach thinks that this state of affairs has already been reached and so theology has had its day and is over. He thought, to be sure, that a naturalised religion, a kind of celebration of our human necessities (such as eating and drinking) would survive—because we would realise that in such celebrations we were actually affirming *ourselves*—but that is a separate issue. Still the history of conceptions of God is epistemically significant because it can be seen as a laying out in thought of the various features of human nature, of our needs, aspirations, and developing powers. The whole process of history is one in which we attribute to this alienated fantasy—the imaginative image of a Being who is utterly different from us / alien to us—what are our own aspired natural powers. What happens historically is what Feuerbach calls an "inversion of subject and object" which we need merely to re-invert to get the original real sense. In Feuerbach's memorable phrase: When we say "God is Love" we *really mean* "Love is divine," that is, that the human capacity to love is a positively valued feature of human nature—a "power" that we wish to cultivate. History then is the story of the way in which we then reappropriate these alienated powers by making them our own and realising that they are our own.

One might well say, or rather one is virtually forced to the thought, that this use of the imagination to create a God was cold comfort at the time, and that it remains cold comfort now. If I want to cross the river, the imaginary idea of a God who can cross the river in my place is no substitute. I think that it is precisely this inadequacy that causes people to hold fast to these imaginative constructs. They are not the objects of obsessive concern *although* they do not work, but precisely *because* in one basic sense they do not work. If they did work they would truly and fully satisfy our need, and would they not then themselves become dispensible? This would seem rather clearly to be the consequence of Feuerbach's reductionist approach to theology and the theological form of activation of the imagination. Once Divine Love may have given our inchoate aspirations a certain structure and direction, but if it is merely a compensatory fantasy, once you have the real thing—once humans really have the power of love for each other—the imaginary form is useless, and at best of historical value. Divine Love, however, was supposed to be both a) something located in an alienated construct of the imagination—God—*and also* b) something *infinite*. Even if one agrees both that the imaginative projection has its origin in real experienced human failure, and if one admits that the localisation of the imagined power (in "God") is a mistake because what are finally at issue are human powers and their development, does this necessarily devalue the aspiration for limitlessness in the development of human powers, for the "infinity" of purportedly divine love? Might not there still be a residue of something which is not completely without value left, a utopian impulse that arises to be sure from finite disappointments, but develops a legitimate life of its own which does not automatically disappear when real human powers progressively unfold?

There seem prima facie to be two further difficulties with Feuerbach's account of a post-theological society. First, an individual may find complete meaningfulness in integration into the productive activity of a collectively organised society, but then again he or she may not. Whether it is likely that such integration will be fully satisfactory to any given individual depends on many empirical factors, including details about how the society is organised, and perhaps features of personal temperament. But even if a social group is optimally well organised, it is not, or should not be, a foregone conclusion that that is what the individual will adopt existing structures of meaning as his or her own. Is he, or she, to be forced? Forced to lead a meaningful life against one's will?

There is also a second objection: this whole discussion, while interesting enough in itself, has focused on only *one* aspect of the original problem and left one important factor out of consideration.

Thinking back to Job, his problems are not overwhelmingly either cognitive (like those analysed by Kant) or social (like those analysed by Hegel and the proto-idealists). Job's problems are not *exclusively* lack of feeling of identification with his society or even lack of developed powers, but the loss of his flocks, boils and pustules on his body, the death of his children, and so forth. Maybe greater power would have allowed Job to keep his flocks intact and save his children from certain well-defined dangers, but no amount of human power will render his body completely invulnerable to illness or his children immortal. It is true about man as much today as it was two thousand years ago that

ἄπορος ἐπ᾽ οὐδὲν ἔρχεται
τὸ μέλλον· Ἄιδα μόνον
φεῦξιν οὐκ ἐπάξεται[12]

He encounters nothing that will confront him which he does not have the means to deal with: the only thing he cannot provide himself with is a way of escaping death.

One might use the term "existential," as opposed to cognitive or sociopolitical, to refer to these concerns. There are actually two slightly distinct issues here, but both of them can be abstractly categorised as relating to human "finitude." In fact, "finitude" is often adopted as a more general description of what it is about human life that makes it unsatisfactory in a way no social reform could change. First, there are forms of concern for fundamental features of human life, such as birth and death, that seem to be rather independent of the particular social, economic, and political order in which we find ourselves, and which are yet not merely atemporal properties of our cognitive apparatus. Many philosophers held that the central "existential" feature of finite human life was "death."[13] The second kind of issue that is often discussed here is one having to do with the inherent nature of human desire and choice. To choose X is not to choose any Y that is not compatible with X, and there is no reason to deny that this represents some kind of limitation inherent to the human condition. We all have to face our own death alone, and no amount of sensible work during my lifetime or social solidarity with my friends and neighbours will completely do away with the need for me to find some way of facing up to this aspect of my finitude, although forms of social organisation can clearly make death more or less bitter. Similarly, it has been argued, despite Marx's early fantasy about a form of society in which I hunt and fish in the morning and write philosophy books in the evening,[14] if I choose to spend the day boxing, I simply will not be able to spend the evening playing the violin. Much of the central part of the intellectual history of Europe during the twentieth century was dominated by disagreements between followers of Feuerbach (for instance, Marx) and existentialists.

Once a connection is established between certain forms of enquiry or intellectual discipline, such as philosophy, with interests or needs, however, the door is open to further subversive thoughts. It might be the case that some particular conceptual or theoretical invention itself creates a set of psychological needs which, once they are in existence, are difficult to get rid of. This is the model that Nietzsche uses for Christianity.[15] It develops a complex set of practices and institutions which arise for perfectly understandable, but utterly contingent, and perhaps slightly disreputable reasons, for instance human weakness and resentment of that weakness, but which, once they get themselves established, generate from within the new set of human needs of which Christianity is the fulfilment. The salvation which Christianity offers is, arguably, not for everyone but for those who need it. Since salvation means in the first instance salvation from sin, so it would seem that the Christian κήρυγμα—the message that sins could be erased and salvation was at hand—would have no purchase on those with no sense of sin. Missionaries have special difficulty with people lacking a sense of sin, so they may need to create one.[16] Christianity did not in the first instance cure the preexisting problem of

sin, but attempted to cure a completely different (and, Nietzsche
thinks, virtually incurable) *other* condition, namely a historically specific widespread form of human illness. Christianity, as he puts it,
"turned sick people into sinners." This means that Christian institutional life can genuinely not merely inculcate a *belief* that one is a
sinner but can actually produce people whose somatic constitution
is one which is correctly described as "sinful." The model here is addiction to drugs. Those who believe or feel themselves to be "sinners"
will think they need the consolations Christianity can provide; those
who really have been turned into sinners really do need that consolation, in the way the addict needs the drug. The only difference is
that whereas we tend to assume that drug addiction is "in principle"
reversible (that is, given sufficient willpower and a facilitating environment), Nietzsche seems to think that for most people the changes
introduced by Christianity will be effectively irreversible. Still, this
is compatible with thinking they are radically contingent.

Nietzsche, then, agrees with Marx that most members of contemporary populations really do have a metaphysical need, but attributes this not to deficient social conditions which cause people to
need consolation for the exhausting but meaningless work to which
they are condemned, but to their own inherent weakness, and the
operation throughout millennia of social institutions which generate
that need. This purported "metaphysical need" for a consoling world
view is a philosophical claim about what people need. One can, of
course, reject the existence of a metaphysical need, while continuing
to accept a general view of human beings which emphasises that they
are beings constituted by various needs (for food, drink, and so forth),
and, of course, one can assert that needs are an important separate
category without asserting that they are the *only* thing that charac-
terises humans. Humans may well have needs, desires, interests, beliefs, and so forth without there being any form of universal reduc-
tion of these to some single category.

Still there is the kernel of something else in this Nietzschean view
that it is important to keep a grip on, and that is his account of the

way in which the imaginative satisfaction of an otherwise unsatisfied need can change what I really need. I try to remedy my weakness by inventing the imaginary consolation of Christianity, but the real operation of the institutions which Christianity in turn develops changes what I need. This may be a positive development, at any rate one which we as the heirs of the change retrospectively judge positively. The "priests" who invent various religious fantasies, after all, in some sense render the human being for the first time an "interesting animal."[17] It is an important fact about the development of human culture that sequences of events like these are possible.

Suppose we clap our hands together to draw the rain god's attention to us. Then we do that rhythmically. Then we sing and dance in rhythm to please him. Since pleasing the god is, we think, very important, we develop more and more complex forms of clapping and singing. Eventually, after four or five thousand years we get the b-minor Mass. It is perfectly possible that we might *not* have got that, had we not had the illusory religious beliefs we had. The music of that mass is made to be as close to being an appropriate, satisfying sound for God to hear as possible, but would also be an appropriate sound for any human of an appropriate level of musical cultivation to hear. It is neither the case that the origin—even the necessary origin—of this music in utterly ridiculous beliefs makes the music any the less beautiful, nor should the fact that we find the music beautiful commit us to endorsing the matrix of beliefs out of which it arose. Perhaps one needs in some circumstances to have aspirations to something beyond what one can ever in fact achieve in order to attain certain high levels of achievement at all. One might here speak of the "utopian" aspirations or a "utopian impulse." Note, too, that one should not be too quick in this area of human life to apply the simple dichotomy between "true belief" / "false belief" (or even "well-supported belief" / "disconfirmed belief"). A lot of the "beliefs" associated with traditional forms of philosophy and religion don't even purport to be descriptive or they are too indeterminate, too lacking in specific propositional content, for us even to say whether or not they are true (or false): "God is an agent who created the world 4500 years ago" is perhaps a statement that can be true or false, but what about "Be perfect even as your heavenly father is perfect" or "There is a destiny that shapes our ends / rough-hew them as we will" or "Ζεὺς γὰρ μεγάλης γλώσσης κόμπους / ὑπερεχθαίρει."[18] An aspiration, such as to make music so perfect it would please even the god, may be more or less ambitious, more or less energising for those who nourish it in themselves, more or less socially useful; it is not obvious that looking for the truth value of the more propositional beliefs perhaps associated with the aspiration is always the best way of attaining any kind of interesting understanding of it.

The word "Utopia" is a coinage of Sir Thomas More, which he used as the title of the book he wrote in Latin and published in 1516. This title is an erudite pun because this invented Latin word could seem to come from one or another of two completely different, also invented, Greek words. In "U + topia," the second component, "τοπία," is straightforward: "place" (in an abstract sense; contrast "τόπος" as a concrete, specific place). However, the first Latin syllable, "U," can either represent the Greek "οὐ," meaning "not," so "utopia" is "no place," or it can represent the completely different word "εὖ," meaning "well" or "good." So Utopia means either a place that is very good or a place that is nowhere, that does not exist in reality, but since it is being discussed at all must exist at least in the imagination, but only in the imagination. In More, and following him the tradition, these two meanings are conflated: It is a place that is too good to be anywhere, too good to exist.

We are all familiar with Marx's criticism of utopian social thinking. There were two prongs of this criticism, one rather superficial, and the other much more deeply rooted. The superficial criticism ran: What is the point of describing the ideal society if one cannot specify a mechanism by which we can act to realise it? Many utopian theorists seem to have accepted a highly naive and very implausible theory of human motivation; that is, they seemed to think that by *describing* a certain state *as good* and recommending it to humans' attention, they have solved the issue of how to attain it. In so doing they over-estimated, he thought, the power which imagining the good actually has to motivate us to act effectively in the world we live in, and also the power which such motivated action might have to attain in the face of a recalcitrant reality, including other agents with their own powers and vested interests, the goals it might actually set itself. The deeper criticism is epistemological rather than practical: utopian thinking assumes that we have too much cognitive ability to detach ourselves from the world we actually live in, to "jump over our own shadow," as Hegel put it. But that is not the case. Every philosopher, even the utopian, is a child of the times, and what looks like utopian speculation about something completely different will eventually show itself to be not so very different at all it will generally turn out to be merely a way of taking some features of the present at face value and absolutising them. Utopian projects, thus, are not so much im-possible to realise; rather they might all too easily be realised and would then, however, turn out to have some of the same basic de-fects of the present, merely magnified.

This all seems perfectly reasonable and unobjectionable, but is not necessarily the last word on utopianism. Consider the work of Gustav Landauer. In 1907 Landauer published a book entitled *Revolution*, which contains a rudimentary anarchist theory of history. In this book he distinguishes two factors in human history: Topia and Utopia. "Topia" is the total state of a society at any given time con-sidered under the aspect of its givenness and *stability*. So one might think of "topia" as a term describing the existing world simply as it now really is. "Utopia," on the other hand, designates all those indi-vidual impulses which under certain circumstances can come to-gether and move this world in the direction of a perfectly func-tioning social formation that "contains no harmful or unjust elements" (". . . Tendenz eine tadellos funktionierende Topie zu gestalten, die keinerlei Schädlichkeiten oder Ungerechtheiten in sich schließt" [". . . a tendency to form an impeccably functioning Topia, which contains within itself no kind of harms or injustices"]).[19] One might bridle at

the inclusion of moralising terms like "*Ungerechtigkeit*" ["injustices"]
in this account, but it is possible to understand this in a historicist
way: at any given time a given population will have (various) conceptions of what is harmful or unjust, and these changing conceptions provide the kernel of the utopian aspiration. The state of affairs
intended in these utopian strivings will not ever be fully realised, and
so their significance consists simply in driving humanity on from one
topia—from one "place"—to the next. However, because they actually do have a kind of motivating force, they are equally not nothing.
At any given point in time, then, Landauer maintains, the utopian
impulses actually and effectively in existence derive from two sources:
specific dissatisfaction with the given topia, and remembrance of all
previous utopias. He puts particular emphasis on the role of history
as a way of revitalising past utopian impulses. He appeals in particular to the twofold sense of the English word "realise," which means
both "come to an understanding of" and "bring into existence." History is supposed to realise previously embodied utopian impulses in
both senses of the word. History, he thought, was at least as much
about creating new forms of cooperative human action, and thus
about the future, as it was about the past. To return to my example
at the start, when people in the late nineteenth century started writing
histories of the Czech nation this was partly a way of producing a set
of institutions in which those who "realised" that they were Czech
(in both senses of the English word) could effectively act so as to
pursue some collective goals which would otherwise be beyond their
reach, in fact creating a Czech nationality rooted in and supported
by a state. I merely note that a theory of this kind might also be
thought to assign to literature a clear function in human life, as the
repository of preserving and clarifying utopian aspirations.

The metaphysical need in the nineteenth century was construed
as essentially retrospective and eirenic. The satisfaction of this need
was to reconcile us with this world in more or less its present form
by showing us that we could see ourselves as integrated into a preexisting metaphysical order. The utopian impulse, by contrast, is future

oriented and polemical. My dissatisfaction with the status quo and recollection of previous moments in history at which similar dissatisfaction has led to effective change is itself directed at a potential future transformation of the present "topia." From the fact that *all* of the content of my utopian striving is not fully "realised" (in the sense of effectively embodied in the world) it does not follow that *any* of that content that did come into existence could have been realised if it had been presented in a non-utopian form. Neither does it follow that whatever transformation eventually does come about is unimportant, because it does not satisfy the utopian impulse fully. Finally, it would also be incorrect to conclude that my retaining my grip on those impulses that are not yet realised or realisable is insignificant. In fact, Landauer is committed to the view that utopian impulses are motivationally essential in permitting any form of human progress or any higher cultural achievement to come about.

> . . . [W]ir dürfen . . . ruhig sagen, daß allen großen Gestaltungen des Mitlebens der Menschen ein Wahn vorgeleuchtet hat, daß die Menschen immer nur durch Wahn aneinander gebunden waren, daß immer nur der Wahn die Individuen zu höheren Organisationsformen und Gesamtheiten aufgebaut hat.[20]

We can say without fear of contradiction that some delusion / obsessive illusion has always gone ahead and illuminated the path to any large form of structuring of human communal life, that humans were ever only bound to one another by some delusion, that only such a delusion ever put together individuals to higher forms of organisation and collectivity.

The word I have translated "delusion / obsessive illusion" here is "*Wahn*," which originally seems to have meant "hope" or "wish," then "wishful thinking, groundless hope," and now in addition carries a very strong connotation of "erroneous, compulsively held conviction."

The relation between those two components in "*Wahn*"—on the one hand, "error," and on the other, "belief compulsively held and acted on"—is unclear. One can, of course, hold an erroneous factual belief and yet not cling to it or act on it compulsively, and one can act compulsively on a belief of indeterminate truth value—"I shall win"—or even on a belief that is true—"There are traces of dust in this room; I must get rid of them *completely* (no matter what the cost)." "*Wahn*" was one of Richard Wagner's favourite terms, and I suspect it was from Wagner's *Meistersinger* that Landauer derived if not the general idea of the cultural productivity of "*Wahn*"—*that* idea goes back to antiquity—at least the use of this specific term for it. At the end of Act II of *Meistersinger* a civic disturbance has broken out in Nürnberg, caused partly by Beckmesser's poor singing and the critical reaction to it by the townspeople, and partly by a complex case of mistaken identity. The next morning, Hans Sachs, the main protagonist, reflects on the previous night's riotous activities, and comes to the conclusion that the whole thing was "*Wahn*," but adds:

> [J]etzt schaun wir, wie Hans Sachs es macht
> daß er den Wahn fein lenken mag,
> ein edel Werk zu tun;
> denn läßt er uns nicht ruhn,
> selbst hier in Nürnberg,
> so sei's um solche Werk'
> die selten vor gemeinen Dingen
> und nie ohn ein'gen Wahn gelingen[21]

[So watch how Hans Sachs carefully guides this obsessive illusion so that it produces a noble work, for, if such illusions never leave us alone, not even here in Nürnberg, it is because works like that that stand out above ordinary things seldom succeed, and if they do succeed never do so with a small admixture of obsessive illusion]

So no b-minor Mass without the obsessive illusion of God, and no Czech Republic without the obsessive illusion in the nineteenth century that there was a naturally given Czech people with a coherent, distinct history. Wagner makes it easy for himself because his Hans Sachs trusts himself to be able to "guide" the development of the illusion "carefully," but, as we know to our cost, in most cases that is not as easy as it looks. There is in fact, one might think, some incompatibility between the very concept of an obsession and the idea that there can be a careful guidance of the way that obsession works itself out. This, however, might, as it were, be a problem for human life, not a problem resulting from some theory, and so might not be a reason to deny the importance of utopian impulses.

I'm suggesting that the metaphysical need and attempts to satisfy it do represent the dead hand of the human past. Perhaps we cannot completely avoid our past; it would be highly surprising if we could, and so it might be perfectly natural for us to be tolerant toward those who still experienced this need in its more vivid forms. Being tolerant does not of course necessarily mean agreeing with them, admitting their claims to truth, or allowing them to impose various of their imaginative structures on others. On the other hand, unless one thinks that we already live in the best of all possible worlds and that lack of flexibility in our relation to our own future is a good thing, giving up our utopian impulses completely would represent a serious loss.

6

Creed, Confession, Manifesto

Pour lancer un manifeste il faut vouloir: A, B, C, foudroyer
contre 1, 2, 3

[To launch a manifesto, it is necessary to want: A, B, C, to
thunder against 1, 2, 3]

Die Kunst gibt nicht das Sichtbare wieder, sondern macht
sichtbar

[Art doesn't reproduce what is visible, but renders visible]

These two short texts, written within a few years of each other, the
first by Tristan Tzara in 1918, the second by Paul Klee in 1920, express in a very succinct way the central intent of any manifesto. A
manifesto, as the name indicates, promises to make something manifest or render something visible. In fact, Klee's statement seems to
be a manifesto raised to the second power: it reveals what art is, and
that is that art reveals (something); one might say that art itself, for
him, is always a kind of manifesto. Tzara points out that a manifesto
is meant to be launched, but launching is a public act which must be
understood relative to the desires, intentions, and goals of those who
formulate and launch it. They are always particularly keen to divide

the world into things they want (A, B, C) and things that are not to be tolerated (1, 2, 3).

Pursuing, then, the parallel between a manifesto and a work of art that is suggested by Klee's remark, what is it exactly that a work of art renders visible? It seems obvious that what is to be rendered visible here is something—whatever it is—which is not (already) visible. What sorts of things, though, are not visible? Several possibilities suggest themselves. First, things can fail to be visible because they are covered over or hidden; either by someone or "by nature." So rendering them visible means revealing or uncovering them.[1] Second, things can fail to be (fully) visible, because, although they are in plain sight, they are, for one reason or another, simply not noticed or attended to. I can render them visible by calling attention to them in an arresting way. Perhaps they are not visible because of general features of space and human perception: either they are too small for the human eye easily to see, or perhaps the context or laws of "perspective" make it difficult to perceive them (from certain points of view). Here decontextualisation, change of perspective, or foregrounding might be ways of rendering them visible. A further possibility is that something is not visible simply because it has not been publicly proclaimed. If I am a vegetarian or a teetotaller, left-handed, arachnophobic, or colour-blind, it is not necessarily that I am "hiding" something; it is perhaps just that if I do not bother to proclaim my state publicly. If so, it will not be "visible." "Invisible," that is, may be shorthand for "impossible, or very difficult to see (for humans) from some particular perspective *and in some medium*" where "medium" refers to such things as, for instance, the kind of light used, the technical methods employed, and so on. Thus, with the invention and the use of infrared light or thermal imaging, things that were not visible (in / through ordinary light) become so. To try to render visible what was before invisible (by using new techniques) or render visible (in some medium) what is inherently invisible (in some other medium) is, therefore, a perfectly coherent endeavour. A further, and perhaps the final, possibility would be to create something completely new and different—whatever that turns out to mean—which *ex hypothesi* cannot have been visible before, because nothing like it ever existed.[2]

This project of "rendering visible" might seem like a high-flown version of the programme which later came to be associated with the architecture of the Bauhaus, an institution of which Klee was a member for many years.[3] The original *Bauhaus-Manifest*, issued by Walter Gropius in 1919, put its main emphasis on the need to overcome the distinction between fine art and craft, and on a return to craftsmanlike values and training, while fully embracing modern industrial materials and methods.[4] Gropius's text is part of the upsurge of socialist thinking that took place in Central Europe at the end of World War I, and it positions itself firmly in that movement with its call for increased social housing, its attack on luxury production as opposed to production for use, and its aesthetics of truthfulness and authenticity. This combination of goals might suggest that at least part of the project of Bauhaus design would be to "reveal" what the new industrial materials now being used "really were," and what they could achieve. So one would do with steel girders what could be done (only?) with steel girders and not use methods derived from building in stone; and one would allow that to be seen. Eventually, and much later, though, commitment to many of the earlier social ideals seems to lapse and affiliation with the Bauhaus came to mean devotion to a particular form of functionalism. Here a clear answer is given to the question what is to be rendered visible: what should be immediately clear to the viewers / users of the building is the function of each item in the work. Sometimes those associated with the Bauhaus spoke as if this was, more or less, the same thing as revealing the "truth about the materials used." A good example might be the Centre Pompidou / Beaubourg in Paris, which puts lifts and other service structures that could only be made of some kind of steel on the outside of what seems to be the surface of the building, making them clearly visible. Why, however, assume that "function" refers either to showing the materials or the role of each formal and structural element in the building rather than, say, the *social* function of the building as a whole? We may have a traditional vocabulary which mandates that Flemish gothic style architectural forms "say" municipal government, Greek revival is for major cultural institutions, and domestic architecture is (vaguely) Georgian (for the aspirational middle class), early Bauhaus (for the wealthy), or Victorian (for the poor). If this set of social meanings were to be firmly in place—a big "if"—buildings could be immediately "read" for their social function, and why shouldn't this form of legibility take priority over the revelation of the truth of the materials used or of the architectural structure?

Perhaps the point is that Klee is speaking not really of *all* art, but of the visual arts. What is music supposed to be making "visible?" It is not impossible to imagine or make up an answer to that, but none of the answers known to me has overwhelming immediate plausibility.

Take the portrait of Churchill by Graham Sutherland (1954), since destroyed by Churchill's family, which, as far as one can tell from the sketches and surviving photos, revealed Churchill very fully and very exactly—his family obviously thought much too fully and too exactly. He is visibly a tired, out-of-touch old man filled with incomprehension and rage at a world he half-realised he no longer understood. After all, by 1954 he must have realised that although the first part of his great project of defeating Hitler *in order to* hold on to the Empire had succeeded, the second part had failed utterly, even if this became uncontrovertibly clear only after Suez, two years later. To speak of art as "making visible" might then refer to the fact that this portrait of Churchill reveals something about its subject, that is Churchill himself, which might not be obvious to spectators still partly dazzled by the successful conclusion of the war in Europe. "Making visible" does not in the first instance mean that the painting reveals something about the painter, the viewer, or the temporary owner(s) (the family who had it destroyed), although that will almost surely also be the case. What it reveals about Churchill will not necessarily be the same thing as what it might tell us about Sutherland, about Churchill's family, or about people who might have viewed the portrait before it was destroyed.

Given that Klee's own art was not really (fully) representational, perhaps one should change tacks here. Perhaps what the portrait is supposed to "make visible" has little to do with the person portrayed. Maybe the "subject" is not Churchill but is to be construed simply as a set of planes, geometric configurations, or patches of pigment. The painting reveals something about them, about what can be done with them, what they lend themselves to, how the tensions between them play themselves out. If the analysis is to apply to music, too, it would seem that it would have to go in this direction. There would have to be something like a (musical) subject about which something is revealed, but what could that be? It does not seem completely far-fetched to say that in some cases a composition can be seen as a process in which a composer takes a certain harmonic, melodic, and rhythmic material and reveals something about that material by showing what can be made of it, and some lovers of music certainly seem to find it illuminating to speak as if an especially satisfying composition showed the potential latent in the material. To be fully satisfied here, one would, however, need to have great confidence that this kind of analysis could be given of more or less all forms of music, rather than of a specially selected range of examples, and one would probably also have to have great confidence that the aesthetic effect was the result of this revelation.

Still, what if one persisted in seeing no special virtue in revealing or making visible over hiding? Thus, Alban Berg thought, precisely contra Bauhaus that each movement of his opera *Wozzeck* should be constructed according to the precise rules of one form or another (fugue, sonata allegro, theme and variations, chaconne), but that he should ensure that the auditors of *Wozzeck* should *not* be able to identify the musical forms being used.[5]

What, then, if one wishes to get fully away from the visual metaphors that are commonly used in thinking about knowledge and about art, and suspects that the persistence and pervasiveness of these metaphors have caused great confusion? Maybe the point of art, religion, or politics (the three areas where manifestos seem most common) is not to make things visible, but something completely different: to change the world, to make life more pleasant, to free people from coercion, to worship a god or protect society, to provide tools for dealing with the human or social environment. There might, in addition, be some things that are better *not* revealed to us.[6]

Up to this point, "revealing," "manifesting," or "rendering visible" has been presented as if it were obvious that what is at issue is a cognitive or epistemic unveiling of something that is ontologically pre-existent, something already there (although not salient). Tzara seems to introduce a completely different dimension into the discussion by mentioning what the members of some group—those issuing the manifesto or identifying with it—*want,* not what they have seen, believe, or know. Desires certainly don't seem to have the same relation to that which exists already as true assertions or propositional beliefs purportedly do. Even if a desire is finally what moves me to action, it is not at all obvious that all desires are connected in any straightforward or one-to-one way with a determinate description of the world in which I find myself. I need not desire some state of the world that is *already* in existence; in fact on a classical analysis,[7] I cannot even really be said to desire something that already exists, because desire is of the nonexistent. If I say I desire something I have already, that means either that I wish to continue to possess it, or I *like* possessing it, which is not at all the same thing.

Whatever the relation between desire and its object, it is, then, not one of pure description. To be sure, the verbal *expression* of a desire, at any rate the explicit formulation of it in a sentence of the form "I want X," can in principle be nothing but the statement of a detached observation, but the observation in question is then one of me, the desirer, and of my state, not of the object desired. Generally, however, if I say "I want tea" I am not reporting anything, but doing something else, such as making a demand or request (although I would generally couch this in a slightly less peremptory way, such as "I would like some tea, please"). Saying that I want a cup of tea is in some contexts a reasonably successful way of obtaining one.

Let us grant that Klee is right and that manifestos are revelations. Tzara adds to this the further qualification that these revelations are promulgated and promoted by people who have a specific agenda of things they do and things they do not want or desire. The proponents of a manifesto have a vested interest in presenting the relation between their revelation and what they desire (and what they do not desire) in a very particular way. They will tend to say they want X, *because,* as they will now reveal, Y is the case. This gives what is, in the modern world, an appropriate structuration: desire grounded on a "realistic" assessment of what is true or how the world is (as revealed). Outside observers may want to turn that relation around. If they are sympathetic, such observers may say that the authors of the manifesto are able to see, and then reveal, Y (only?) because they already wanted X. Desire opened their eyes to something which may have been there already, but which they would otherwise not have been able to see. If the observers are unsympathetic, they are more likely to say that the only reason the authors of the manifesto believe that X is the case, is because they think that if enough others also believe that, their own heart's desire (Y) will be fulfilled. This is a kind of wishful thinking.

As far as the promulgation of the revelation is concerned, it might be useful to think of comparisons with the ancient world. Ancient Greece and Rome contained lots of what we now call "mystery religions," that is forms of ritual in which purportedly hidden, but existentially significant truths were revealed to specially prepared initiates. Access to these rituals was controlled; the preparatory sacrifices were often very expensive, and there was no sense in which they were, or were intended to be, open to all. It was usual for the "revelation" (ἐποπτεία) to take place in secret, for instance in underground chambers, or in dark or otherwise inaccessible places. There was often even a specific prohibition about speaking of anything associated with the rituals (τὰ ἄρρητα), which one could be seriously punished for violating. Revealing the content of the Eleusinian mysteries to a non-initiate was a capital offense in Athens.[8] In stark contrast to this, a manifesto is intended to be "launched" into the full light of day. To "launch" a manifesto, however, is not simply to act in the anodyne sense in which saying anything at all in public is doing something, but to perform a very particular kind of speech act which depends on particular institutional structure and has constituent consequences. To launch a manifesto is closer to saying "I concede defeat" at the end of an election, "I accept these conditions" in a formal negotiation, or "I plead guilty" in court than to, say, merely reading out the temperature on a thermometer, speaking out the Latin name of a tree I happen to pass, or reading out the headline in a newspaper I see displayed.

The further characteristic of a manifesto which Tzara points out is the striking importance for writers of manifestos of what they are *against*. The fulmination against 1, 2, 3 is at least as important as the positive wanting of A, B, C. Even in the phrase cited from Klee, it is striking that the *negative* part of the statement comes before the positive. What is really important and must be noted first is what Klee rejects: art as *imitation* of what is antecedently visible.

Sometimes the negative part of the manifesto can become so complex, extensive, and baroque that it outruns the positive part. A careful study of any of the standard collections of early creeds of the Christian churches, such as Denziger-Schönmetzer's *Enchiridion symbolorum definitionum et declarationum de rebus fidei et morum* (editio xxxvi, Herder, 1965), will illustrate this clearly. The earliest creed (Denziger 125), the "Nicene Creed" of AD 325,[9] contains a dozen or so short and simple positive items: belief / faith in god, the church, the forgiveness of sin and the resurrection of the flesh (σαρκός ἀνάστασις), followed by a handful of beliefs that are specifically anathematized (that is, condemned as pernicious and to be rejected). In the course of time creeds mutate into documents that trail behind them enormous swathes of anathemas (Denzinger 152–180; 187–208; 250–264; 421–438 *et passim*]. Some people who were young in the sixties will remember similar phenomena among groups on the political left, when every clause of a statement seemed to be followed by four or five qualifications about what that clause certainly did *not* mean, the qualifications being set up specifically to exclude what were thought to be the typical beliefs of potentially rival groups.

This reference to religious creeds seems appropriate. Up to now, to be sure, I have been treating both Tzara's text and that of Klee as instances of "manifestos," but Klee's text is not actually called a "manifesto." Rather it was published in a collection called *Schöpferische Konfessionen*. "*Konfession*" here obviously does not mean "confession" in the usual sense of that word in English—admission of some failing or sin—but rather in the sense in which one speaks of the "Augsburg Confession" ("*Bekenntnis*"), which was a document presented to the Emperor Charles V in 1530 by Protestant princes setting out the tenets of their religious faith. So Klee's "*Konfession*" is a kind of creative creed or credo.

A "creed" is a Christian invention of a rather peculiar kind. In 325 the Roman Emperor Constantine, freshly converted to Christianity, convoked and presided over a council of church leaders (bishops) at Nicaea in what is now Turkey. His intention was to get public agreement on a canonical form of belief for the church as a whole. One can ask why it was thought appropriate for the Emperor to have anything at all to do with a statement of religious beliefs. This does, however, solve one major question, which often plagues public statements, namely by what authority is the statement made? Here the authority is, on the one hand, that of the collected bishops, but, much more importantly, that of the Emperor. So a creed is a set of beliefs collectively and authoritatively agreed on, which define a group (Christian Church) and are mandatory for its members.

As far as I can determine, there is no very clear semantic distinction between the words "creed" and "confession" in English, if only because "confession" is generally used in a different sense altogether ("confession of sins"). If one took the etymology seriously, it would be tempting to try to make a distinction between the two of the following sort. A "creed" is a matter of individual belief (*credo*), whereas a confession is a public statement (individual or collective: *confiteor*, *confitemur*). However, perhaps perversely, I am going to adopt a usage in the rest of this chapter which is almost the reverse of this. That is, I shall tend to use "creed" for a public, collective document like the Nicene Creed, and "confession" for more informal and personal statements of belief.

What a confession reveals about the world is, at the very least, where the confessor stands, like Luther at the Diet of Worms (1521). The tale told about this event may be apocryphal. Complex theological debates had, of course, been conducted before Luther made his powerful and striking statement, and they would continue to take place later, but these are downplayed in the *story*, which is told as one of a moment of virtually pure performance. When the inquisitor asks the simple question "Will you recant and submit to the authority of the church?" the answer is an equally simple, but high-octane and absolute refusal. "No, I can no other. Here I stand." This contrasts strikingly with the voluble and versatile discoursing, the filigree dialectic, the citation of arguments and counterarguments that constitute the drama of, for instance, the trial of Socrates.[10] Is there, one might ask, some connection between the existence of a creed and monotheism?

In the ancient world, two different things that can both be called, in a crude and general sense, "monotheism" arose in the eastern Mediterranean. There is, first of all, a positive philosophical view which one might call "monotheism arising out of speculation." Then there is another kind of view, which puts more emphasis on the politics of refusal, negation, and exclusion, and which one might call "monotheism arising out of henotheism." The positive philosophical monotheism is one of the offshoots of the Greek search for an ἀρχή, some kind of explanatory and organisational principle that would allow a synoptic comprehension of everything there is. Xenophanes drew the conclusion that finally there would have to be one, and only one, such principle.[11] If you call it "God" that would mean (finally) one god. This was the important point and what one then did with the plurality of visible gods, worshipped in the various cities of the Mediterranean world, was merely a further detail of no great theoretical or moral importance. There might be some *stories* about the gods that needed to be refuted, but that was a separate issue. As far as we can tell, this form of monotheism was considered to be perfectly compatible with remaining relaxed about continuing to participate in a variety of cults of individual recognised deities. Maybe they were aspects (or "mere aspects?") of the one final explanatory principle, a god, who in any case might not turn out to be anything like a human individual. In fact, the more one thought about it, the less likely the final explanation would be anything like a person at all. Rather it would be like a λόγος, an abstract rational structure. Maybe the individual gods of cult were something like sub-gods, maybe they were literary aides-memoires, or pleasing and useful inventions designed to hold cities together and indispensable for that purpose, maybe they were just powerful natural forces, or heroes whose memory deserved to be cultivated. Maybe the gods were the biggest or most powerful possible *persons* in the universe, and going up scale beyond them you arrived at a philosophically more interesting final abstraction ("the One," "the idea of the good," "the *logos*") of huge explanatory value, but little potential relevance to everyday human life, because one could not propitiate "it" or appeal to it for help. Perhaps the answers to these questions were not really that important, so one could leave the whole issue open. Why, in any case, should "the One" be at all interested in what opinions we had about it, in our actions or in our prayers? Epicureans thought that gods probably existed but, because they were perfect beings, had no interest in human affairs at all.[12] Even if people do confuse the gods worshipped on earth with the cosmic principle, what is so wrong with that? People make lots of philosophical mistakes all the time, so enlighten them. It isn't obvious why speculative errors need to be repressed or those who commit them punished.[13]

Henotheistic monotheism has a very different structure.[14] Henotheism is the worship of only one god by an individual or group. This, of course, is a completely different thing from speculative monotheism, because worship is a question of some form of overt action, not of belief. One can in principle easily worship one god, that is to cultivate him (or her) exclusively, without (necessarily) believing that there is only one god, just as a Roman young man was expected to exhibit special obedience to his father's wishes without thereby thinking that his was the only father who existed, or just as one might think that anyone who marries should marry only one person without thinking that only one person existed in the world who was a "spouse." To worship "one god" here means inherently *not* to worship any of the competitors, and since such competitors might well exist, this is not at all an empty demand. One might develop a repressive apparatus, either an ideational one or even a real one, to punish those of "his" worshippers who deviate from the ethical and political demand to worship only the correct one god.

What happens, though, when inflationary pressures begin to afflict a henotheistic tradition? This tendency toward gigantism may be thought to reach its climax when some begin to believe that their god is bigger and better than that of others,[15] so everyone should worship just him. In addition, the god, being of an irascible disposition, might be incensed if his followers do not worship only him. One way of exalting the henotheistic deity is by denigrating his competitors. However, a limit is passed when one moves from "This god is the only one to worship, and we will sanction you to the extent to which we can, if you refuse or deviate and whore after some other god" to a kind of henotheism transmuted into a speculative principle about the *existence* of gods. At that point, "Don't worship them; they are not the right gods for us to worship" becomes "Do not worship them; *our* god is the ἀρχή, and, what's more, *they don't exist*," and henotheism has become a kind of monotheism. When that happens, the theological problems with rendering such a position coherent increase exponentially.

If speculative monotheisms are matters of the right belief, and henotheistically based monotheisms are more focused on forms of worship, that is external cult, distinguishing correct from incorrect forms, and on repressing external deviance, the Christian notion of

a "creed" adds a possible third dimension, that of internal orientation, attitude, psychic state. The basic term of a Christian creed,
"*credo*" (πιστεύω), does not refer directly to a state of propositional
belief, nor to a specific form of external cult practice.

Earlier a creed was described as a set of the defining beliefs by
virtue of which people were members of a certain group, and this is
the way in which Christianity usually portrays itself. However, if one
looks at them closely, most of the creeds in their fully developed form
(say the Creed of Nicaea)[16] seem to be a mixture of elements and, in
addition, of elements of different types, not all of which are beliefs
in the cognitive sense. Some, to be sure, are assertions of purported
truths, but others are expressions of trust or of hopes,[17] speculations,
performances of varying kinds. What does seem to be clear is that
creeds are not originally in every respect merely lists of propositions
to be affirmed. "I (we) believe in one god" is not in the first instance
intended to be the answer to a speculative question of the form "How
many gods are there?" but to the completely different question "In
what / whom do you place your final trust?"; or perhaps we would be
more likely to say "What form does your final commitment in life
take?" It may, of course, be that for such belief / trust / faith to make
sense, certain things are presupposed to be true of the world, but asserting something and presupposing something in what one says are
two completely different things. "I believe in the catholic church,"
one of the invariable components of all the oldest creeds, does not
even have the right linguistic form to express a propositional belief.
"I believe in the resurrection of the corpses,"[18] on the other hand, is
not what we would call an expression of confidence or trust, but
something like a (pious) hope.

As time goes by, church authorities tried not simply to formulate
matters of commitment, but to express fully the assumptions that are
(or ought correctly to be) made by such professions of faith and commitment. Political agents, such as the Roman Emperor, had an
equal interest in control of this. The history of creeds is a compli-

cated texture of struggles between religious experts and political institutions in the cause of finding formulae that would both survive minimal logical scrutiny and have some chance of being widely accepted (more or less freely, depending on the means of coercion available) by the members of the target group, "the faithful."

Creeds do several things at the same time. Vis-à-vis the outside world they express and reveal to others the characteristic or defining commitments of the group and help it distinguish itself from others, something which, in view of the henotheist background of Christianity, is an essential part of it. Vis-à-vis individual members of the group, they set the terms of membership, and define and reveal to members the identity they have assumed in joining, or being otherwise incorporated into, the group. The act of reciting the creed is often thought to strengthen group solidarity and also to have a magical character. To say the words is to bring it about that they are true.[19]

That this person standing in this river or cistern or at this baptismal font or pool undergoes the operations, performs the required deeds, and says the words will reveal lots of things, and by revealing them may bring other things about. To be sure, one must remember the example given by Max Weber and see that what exactly it reveals is socially complex. As Weber noticed,[20] when in North Carolina (in the United States) a certain aspiring banker was baptised into some Protestant sect in a very public ceremony, this might tell one less about his piety than about his greed. Also, since the sect was well known for its view that only the elect and righteous could be baptised, and its elders were known to make diligent enquiries about rectitude (including fiduciary rectitude) and available capital resources before permitting him before to be baptised, the fact that he was allowed to go forward with the ceremony showed that he had survived the scrutiny. The members of the sects would themselves do their banking with him, and, since he had now become "one of them," would protect him potentially in other ways, too. They had certified him; his reputation was established, and, for the moment at least,

assured, so his credit would be good. Reciting the words and per-
forming the deeds that constituted baptism, in this context, made
him creditworthy.

This is one of the differences between a proper full-blooded creed
and a manifesto. Manifestos are not usually recited collectively in
public or intended to be so recited; even if they are collective manifestos, they are creeds for a disenchanted, secular world. In addition,
their position in the existing relations of political power is characteristically different from those in which creeds arise. Creeds formalise
existing power relations: the Emperor and the dignitaries of the
church are *there* in Nicaea, laying down the law of belief; they address an existing group. Manifestos nowadays are usually issued from
more politically marginal positions and are a call to come together
and maintain solidarity around a certain set of beliefs. They address
an audience that does not yet exist as fully organised and they appeal to a "*communauté à construire*" rather than to an existing group.
Finally, the form of negativity (that against which the creed / manifesto "thunders" [*foudroyer*]) is different. The creed excludes heretics
from an existing group; a manifesto is much more likely to take the
form of a tacit critique of some existing state of the world.

Both manifestos and creeds differ from "apologiae" in that the later
are inherently argumentative,[21] whereas the former are assertive and
performative. However, a discursive defence of given theses or of a
mode of life is something very different from the bald or incantatory
statement of faith, trust, and beliefs, or the various performative acts
which one finds in manifestos and creeds. The real authority behind
a traditional creed is the collective expertise and power of religious
and secular dignitaries (originally the bishops at Nicaea and the Emperor). Such a creed usually claims to have sources further back than
that, in the revelation of the deity himself (or herself or themselves).
A modern manifesto cannot appeal to those sources, so what kind of
authority can it have? One possibility, to move for a moment outside
the realm of art, is that it can appeal, as in the case of the manifesto
of Marx and Engels, to "science" as purportedly relatively impartial

and unprejudiced.[22] Another possibility is that in "democratic" societies a manifesto can claim to have some authority if it succeeds in being recognised as revealing and articulating the world view, beliefs, commitments of some significant section of the electorate. Or perhaps art reveals something in a way that gives it its own inherent authority.[23]

Individual confessions are, then, not manifestos, and the latter shared with ancient creeds at any rate the aspiration to formulate the identifying traits of a human group, and thus to be the voice of a collectivity. To be sure, here, as in so many other cases, Dada seems a kind of exception. Tzara writes "les vrais dadas sont contre DADA" ["True dadaists are against DADA"],[24] but I submit that this is really a confirmation of the view that the point of a manifesto is to formulate a collective aspiration. The statement is intended to be outrageous and would not be so if we did not see it as stating a kind of paradox. Given that the Dadaists were, in some sense, trying to be a club without rules,[25] any manifesto they released would have to be at the same time an anti-manifesto.

With an individual creative confession the question of authority also arises in a very different way, since in a confession I am not trying to subject you (perhaps with a little help from my friend the Emperor) to a creed, nor trying to mobilise you around a manifesto. Whatever authority a confession might have would derive primarily from the power and success of the works I produce. I can take the Nicene Creed seriously for any number of reasons: the accumulated weight of history and the significance of this document in that history, the authority of generations of Emperors and bishops, the consent of the faithful, perhaps I may even believe it is divinely inspired. I take Klee's confession seriously because of Klee's paintings.

The 1920 volume *Schöpferische Konfessionen*, from which Klee's remark which was cited at the beginning of this essay is derived, also contained a "creative confession" by the composer Arnold Schönberg, which is entitled (ironically) "Certitude."[26] In this essay Schönberg warns how easy it is for an artist to observe (and then describe) his own practice incorrectly,[27] and says that in his case the only thing he can be sure of is that whatever he finally comes up with will be very different from whatever he originally envisaged. This, of course, undermines the very idea of a creative confession. If Klee is a bad observer of himself and his creative processes, why should admiration of his painting lead anyone to attribute any free-standing authority to his self-description in the "Confession?" The "Confession" then becomes a curio or a symptom or something else. Self-reflective as ever, Schönberg goes on to say that any "certainty" he has, is one he has only "today," with the implication that it could change tomorrow. He concludes his remarks with one of those wonderfully sardonic comments that seemed to come so easily to him, saying that it would be easy for him to issue a manifesto (he calls it a "programme" but that is an unimportant verbal difference) for *other people* to observe, provided, of course, that he was free to ignore it. If others realised the "programme," so much the better: it would dispense him even from the necessity of feeling guilty about not following it at all.

Although he published a book in 1924 entitled *Sept manifestes DADA,* Tzara says he does not like "principles" or manifestos;[28] neither do I (recalling that not every collection of assertions is a manifesto, but only one with a collective intention standing in a highly specific social context). We would, I think, be better off, if the particular performative and functional social niche, which manifestos fill (in varying ways) did not exist. So is that my (wholly negative) creed? I forbear to point out the obvious pragmatic contradiction, which I, too, have not failed to notice in this. It is not, however, the mere contradiction that bothers me. After all, in my view, mental life does not consist simply in contemplating or eternally reaffirming a fixed set of demonstrably true propositions but exists only as a form of motion and activity, where contradictions are an inevitable part of the vital movement.[29]

Tzara, in fact, had already found a way, when he "launched" the Dada Manifesto of 1918, to undermine the world of the manifesto very effectively, arguably even more effectively than in the text of 1918.

He did this on July 14, 1916, when he read out to one of the first Dada meetings at the Café Voltaire in Zürich his "La première aventure céléste de Monsieur Antipryne" ["The first celestial adventure of Monsieur Pyrine"], which was later reprinted as "Manifeste de Monsieur Pyrine."[30] This text begins:

Dada est notre intensité: qui érige les baïonnettes sans conséquence la tête sumatrale du bébé allemand

[Dada is our intensity: which erects the bayonets without consequence the Sumatran head of the German baby][31]

July 14 was not only Bastille Day, but in 1916 it fell during the height of the battles for Verdun and on the Somme on the Western Front, and the so-called Brussilow Offensive on the Eastern Front.[32] Given the circumstances, one might have been forgiven for thinking, as the recitation started, that what was being performed was a kind of *l'art pour l'art* or even explicitly antiwar text. "You with your tanks, phosgene-gas shells, artillery, and bayonets have *your* intensity; we, Dadaists, have our own intensity, but our bayonets are not lethal. . . ." One might wonder whether *"sans consequence"* here means "without having any concrete results" or "incoherently," but this is part, as if were, of the "usual" ambiguity of meaning permitted, even encouraged, in poetic contexts. However, at this point Tzara abandons grammar and the usual forms of logic, and simply hangs on to the sentence a further noun and adjective with a dependent genitive (la tête sumatrale du bébé allemand) without specifying how that should be attached to and in what relation it stands to what went before. Does this phrase stand in apposition to what went before ("érige les baïonnettes . . .<ainsi que> la tête . . ." ["erects bayonets, <as well as raising> the head of the baby"]), or is there a missing preposition that is notionally to be supplied ("érige les baïonnettes . . .<contre> la tête . . ." ["erects bayonets <pointed against> the head of the baby"] or "érige les baïonnettes sans conséquence <pour> la tête . . ." ["erects bayonets which are without consequence <for> the head of the baby"])? What does Sumatra have to do with all of this, anyway? Once one starts, the possibilities are almost infinite. It is as if a bayonet, the moment it was mentioned, cut off intellectual coherence and the logical sequencing of thought (*consequence*), but the stump remaining bleeds enormous amounts of possible continuations. Tzara continues:

> Dada est la vie sans pantoufles ni parallèles; qui est contre et pour l'unité et décidément contre le futur;

> [Dada is life without house-slippers and parallels; which is against and for unity and decidedly against the future;]

After the semicolon the sentence alternatingly limps on and leaps forward, ending with an enthusiastic exhortation: ". . . et crachons sur l'humanité" [". . . and let's spit on humanity"]. The whole text ends with a fervent: "je vous adore."

If Nietzsche is right that we shall not get rid of god until we get rid of grammar,[33] Tzara makes a very good start.[34] He does not announce, assert, or *say* that he is abandoning grammar, or that logic has become irrelevant; he just *does* whatever it is he is doing in this sentence, and by doing it, manifests more vividly than any general announcement could, the end of the grammatical era. It is as if Klee, instead of writing his "Confession," had painted a picture which did not reproduce anything already visible, but simply rendered something visible.

Perhaps I should say I stand with Tzara and Schönberg, except that Tzara does his best to undermine the very idea of a fixed location and Schönberg does not know where he is, and, even if that were a fixed location, he assumes he will be leaving it any minute.

7

Ivan Is Unwell

In book I of his *Histories,* Herodotus tells the story of Solon, an Athenian renowned for his wisdom and good judgment, and the exceedingly wealthy and powerful king Croesus of Lydia.[1] While Solon was visiting Sardis, the capital of Lydia, Croesus showed him all his wealth and his many possessions and then asked him disingenuously who, in his opinion, was the happiest person in the world. This was obviously not a serious question, and Herodotus says as much; rather it was a way for Croesus to fish for compliments and get the sage to give a positive, authoritative judgment on him as leading the most satisfying, the most enviable, the most praiseworthy life imaginable. Actually, Croesus, in Herodotus's account, slightly stacks the deck in his own favour because in asking the question, he uses a word for "happy" which has a strong secondary connotation of "prosperous" or even "wealthy" (ὀλβιώτατος)—actually in grammatical form a superlative, "extremely wealthy." He is then all the more disappointed when Solon names various people of rather modest circumstances, whom he has never heard of, but who lived useful lives, died, and were well remembered by their friends. Solon makes two points. First he claims that, given the many and varied accidents to which human life is subject, it is not possible to give a definitive judgment of the kind Croesus seeks on a human life before the person in question has died, because presumably such a judgment should be of the life *as a whole*. This in itself should be sufficient to render impossible the worldly self-satisfaction that seems to have been endemic among some in ancient societies, or at any rate that was particularly targeted by ancient moralists, and which is not unknown even nowadays. By extension, it would also be likely to make it more difficult to maintain the moral self-righteousness which was one of Jesus's particular bêtes noires and which has come down in the Christian tradition as the despised character flaw of "Pharisaism." The "Pharisee" is contemptible because he glories in his own righteousness. Solon's second point is that one should not rush to attribute the greatest overall happiness either to those who have the most visible external prosperity, to those who are most celebrated or envied, or, finally to those who seem most pleased with themselves at any given moment. In fact, as Herodotus continues the story, Croesus lost his kingdom and all his wealth and barely escaped execution by combustion at the hands of Cyrus the Great, who defeated him and incorporated the kingdom of Lydia into the empire which Cyrus was in the process of creating.

In a text written fifteen hundred years later, Dante's *Divine Comedy*,[2] the main character in the poem encounters two of his political and military opponents, father and son: Guido and Buonconte da Montefeltro. The first, Guido, resides in hell. He is depicted as having had very considerable foresight in conducting his life on earth; after an active youth devoted to war and trickery, he joined the Franciscan order as a mendicant to make amends for his many sins. He seems to have been a perfectly unexceptional Franciscan, so that his strategy had every appearance of being successful. The angels were already preparing to escort him on his death to the realm of the blessed. However, toward the end of his life he falls into a trap. The Pope asks him for good advice, and, following Catholic doctrine, cites Matthew 16.19, which is interpreted as meaning that he, the Pope, has the power to forgive sins. To entice Guido to give him effective advice, the Pope offers to absolve him of any sin he might commit in giving this advice, in advance, and Guido then counsels the Pope that the best way forward for him is to make a promise which he has no intention of keeping. The Pope follows the advice and things work out marvellously (for him). However, when Guido comes to die, devils drag him down to hell. One of them explains to him that, although it is true that the Pope has the power to absolve sins, this power will work only on those who truly repent of their sins; since Guido gave the Pope the advice to act just in the way he, Guido, had acted before taking the habit of a Franciscan, this showed that he had not truly repented. Devils may be evil, but they are not necessarily stupid. This particular devil is, in fact, a supremely gifted logician (Forse / tu non pensavi ch'io löico fossi, ll. 122–123). So becoming a Franciscan availed Guido nothing and he is discovered by Dante burning in one of the lower reaches of the inferno, the place for those who are irremediably damned (canto XXVII).

Buonconte, son of Guido, seems also to have lived a life devoted to highly organised rapine and pillage; yet when he dies, he enters Purgatory, a temporary place of purification, with a positive prospect of eventually attaining paradise. He was saved, Dante recounts, because when fleeing from the battle in which he had been mortally wounded, he died with the name "Maria" on his lips. The very beautiful but exceptionally long description of how Buonconte was rolled around and died in the mud among the reeds emphasises that he died *alone,* so no human heard the perhaps barely perceptible last sigh from his lips, but in any case the articulation of the words was not important; the intention, as in the case of Guido, was. The strong impression is given that this invisible shift, this repudiation of all that he has been at the very last moment of life, is sufficient for his salvation. What makes all the difference to his life is not the extreme variability of external circumstances, as in the case of Croesus, but an externally imperceptible shift in the inner state of the soul.

The third example is Tolstoy's *The Death of Ivan Ilyich.*[3] As he gradually declines and dies, the eponymous protagonist reflects on the life he has led and finds it overall unsatisfactory, although it has been outwardly perfectly successful in most conventional terms. What is

striking about the novella is that it describes the way in which Ivan
Ilyich becomes disillusioned with all the standards he had used and
which he still has available to him for judging human actions, behaviour, and forms of life. They dissolve for him into nothingness
and illusion. In this regard, his case forms a complete contrast with
the work of Dante. Wherever in hell Dante's damned are located, he
never gives any sense that he, or they, were confused in this regard.
Guido knew, or as we would say "thought he knew," that giving the
advice he gave to the Pope was "good" (liable to be effective) and also
"bad" (the wrong thing to do, damnable). If he hadn't known it was
bad, he would not have insisted on anticipatory absolution. The conflict is a "mere" conflict between the application in the real world of
two standards, both of which are clear and, as it were, valid in their
own way. Dante also holds that the religious standard which prohibits
lying (and, a fortiori, advising people to lie) has priority, but that is
not seen to have any effect on the clarity of the two standards or on
their grip on human life. It remains only for Machiavelli to call into
question this priority, and *The Prince* virtually writes itself. For Tolstoy's Ivan Ilyich, however, everything, including his ideas of good
and bad, right and wrong, lose their shape and their hold on him,
and he feels at sea, dissatisfied but unsure why. It isn't even clear, at
the end, whether he fails to understand his life, or whether he disap-
proves of what it has been, or whether he simply feels that something
important has been left out. It is not at all clear *why* exactly it has all
been so unsatisfactory. Perhaps what is really unsatisfactory is not his
previous life, but the fact that he now is dying. That would be understandable enough. This, however, is not the construction Ivan puts
on the situation, and probably also not the construction Tolstoy put
on it either. It does seem rarther clear, though, that within the terms
set by the novel itself, Ivan had been wrong about his life before.
When young, he *thought* the life he was living was a good one, but
that was not the case. Why assume that at the end of his life he suddenly gets things right? Why should he not *still* be wrong, or be wrong
again (in a different way from before)? In a sense, Ivan cannot be

wrong at the end, because he is not a real person, merely a product of Tolstoy's mind, and he is what Tolstoy says he is. However, once Tolstoy presents his novella to the world, *we*, his readers, can certainly judge the imaginatively created situation and the fictional character differently than Tolstoy wanted us to. If we assume, though, that Ivan's life has all been wrong, even if he cannot say exactly why, this indeterminacy is different from that in the cases of Croesus—it is not hard to understand the unsatisfactoriness of lying on a huge pyre waiting to be burnt alive—or Buonconte, who knew he had lost the battle (the "last battle" for him) and who would also clearly have been disappointed to be confronted with an eternity of living death in a *boglia* in one of the lower reaches of hell.

In the 1940s the German philosopher Theodor Adorno fled Nazi Germany and went to live in the United States, eventually settling in California. He was struck by an odd feature of life there: a very highly developed form of technical rationality (the production of atomic bombs, rudimentary electronic calculating devices, aircraft) was conjoined with a complete absence of anything he could recognise as a valuable indigenous culture, and the inhabitants seemed to lack entirely an autonomous inner life that went beyond a gushing but primitive sentimentality. The resulting vacuum is filled, he thought, by simply using visible external signs of (primarily economic) success, and these alone were used to evaluate a human life. What is perhaps even more striking, this process is fully internalised by the agents themselves, so that they do not realise that something is missing. In one of the books he wrote to analyse this phenomenon, *Dialektik der Aufklärung*,[4] he cites the, for him, very unusual phenomenon of a person incapable of seeing his own life in any other than completely external terms: "'I am a failure' the American says 'and that is that.'"

Adorno's American intends to express a definitive and categorical evaluative judgment about his life as a whole. He says, however, "I am a failure and that is that," rather than, for instance, "my life has been [or, is] a failure." The later formulation might seem to leave open the possibility of distinguishing between the externalities of a human life, its occupational projects, social standing, reputation, status, and so forth, on the one hand, and some "inner core" of the self, on the other. Perhaps one could find traces of the place where this wedge might be inserted between these two sides in the story of Buonconte Montefeltro: his whole life is a mess, but there remains some small spark of hidden deep insight that is sufficient to motivate the final unheard exclamation which saves his soul; his life was a failure, but he is saved. If "my life was a failure" now has a slightly nineteenth century ring, "I am a failure" speaks rather in the accents of 1940s America. The more contemporary way of putting this would probably be "I am a loser." To call someone "a loser" was to apply an expression that was employed occasionally, but only very sporadically, before the 1980s, when its use suddenly burgeoned. The implication is that it is not merely a matter of contingency that someone's life is a failure; it is a necessary consequence of who that person is, or rather, given the ideological pressure in an economic system like ours to say that failure is "one's own fault," it is a matter both of a kind of necessity *and also* of an inherent moral flaw. The "loser" is someone *defined* by the basic moral flaw of failing to grasp with sufficient initiative and exploit with adequate force and cleverness the ample opportunities for self-advancement which the society provides.

To return to Ivan Ilyich, Tolstoy writes that at the end of his life Ivan Ilyich was able to tell himself the story of his life. He told it as a story of failure, although he can never really articulate the reason it was a failure. The point of Ivan Ilyich's story, though, it has always seemed to me, is not so much that at the end for the first time he can tell the story of his life as a whole; the whole story suggests that this was something he could always do, had he wanted to; it is just that his narrative, like his life, would have been conventional, banal, and boring. His life was *trop comme il faut* to be at all interesting. Neither is the main point that he now sees his life differently and clearly, although that is what he (and perhaps Tolstoy, too) might think. Rather, the shocking thing at the end is that Ivan understands that the narrative *does not matter*. In the end, *all this does not matter*. This does not mean that at age twenty "all this" did not matter to Ivan

Ilyich. Since, to repeat, Ivan does not exist and never existed except as a literary creation of Tolstoy, the only reasonable meaning one can give to this question is whether Tolstoy represents "all this" as mattering to him. He says it did, so it did (unless I, as reader, have some overwhelmingly strong reason I can give for disagreeing with Tolstoy on this point). Nor that "all this" did not matter to him at age forty; it probably did, although the actual content of "all this" had probably changed for him between the ages of twenty and forty. That is all there is: sometimes things mean something; then they don't; sometimes observers can hazard a guess about "causal" connections; sometimes they cannot. Is it *obvious* that a person's judgment must be sharpest and most correct at the moment of death? Even if he is wasting away and losing his faculties? Maybe he was wrong at the end and the great obsession with getting ahead in the world, good food and drink and sex, which motivated him in his twenties, was really the right way to life his life. Maybe this correct insight was just covered over by the length of years, or he could no longer grasp its truth when he came to die. Perhaps he simply got too old to enjoy the pleasures of a man of twenty. Or perhaps his view of life at age twenty isn't "right," but it is no more wrong than the views he develops on his deathbed. Or perhaps it is just the case that what suits one in one's healthy twenties will not necessarily suit one equally well in one's sixties if they are spent in ill health or in the senility of one's seventies. Last words and last thoughts are not invariably those most replete with human wisdom. If this seems to be the case, it is because unmemorable ones are nor remembered. Ivan Ilyich is a literary character, so his last words, or rather last thoughts, are nothing beyond what Tolstoy tells us they are: "Death is done for; it is no more" ("Кончена смерть. . . . Её нет болше"), meaning by this presumably that my own death is something I experience only in anticipation, in approaching it, and of course, when I am "there," there is no "me" and hence no death to be approached. If, however, he had been a real human being, he might have died slightly earlier than he is represented as having done. Then his last words and thoughts would have been "Ow, ow, ow" ("У! У! У!") "in different intonations" ("на разные интонации"), which would have been an end more typical of the death of very many human beings, perhaps a majority especially before the advent of anaesthetics.

To continue this fantasy, *if* Ivan Ilyich were to be, or had been, a real human being, rather than a character in fiction, and there were to be an external observer of him, for instance, if I, in 2019, were to observe him (who died sometime, let us assume, in the nineteenth century), I could judge that these things are meaningful and important to him at age twenty; these (perhaps some other) things at age forty, and these (perhaps yet again other things) just before he died. I can, if I wish, put together the whole of his life in one way or another, can judge that he was right about his evaluation of his own life when he was forty, but mistaken at twenty, and also mistaken later on his deathbed. Of course, I can also form a judgment on him that is based on completely different considerations than any he would have had access to. That might be morally dubious, or impolite, or non-empathetic, or "paternalistic," or something—we don't really have a word for this judgment which simply ignores everything about a person's own beliefs, values, and judgments about themselves and their life in making our own assessment of it—but it is not impossible. One can *call* this a "narrative" evaluation, if one wishes, but it need not be. I may judge that Ivan Ilyich was a nineteenth-century property owner, *therefore* a person of whose life one should disapprove—actually, this is not far from the view Tolstoy himself sometimes expressed, at any rate later in *his* life. I can make this evaluation in the face of an assessment of what I take to be his "whole life." He, Ivan Ilyich, will never be in this position, because as long as he is capable of making any assessment at all, he will have to be alive, which means, as has been shown, that he does not have his full life in front of him as an object of judgment. He can make a judgment on an imaginary object—his life including the parts of it which he has not yet lived—but that is a judgment on a different object.

"Success" and "failure" are inherently contextual concepts. In addition, "Was Caesar's life a failure?," "Is Henry Kissinger's life a failure?" (asserted while Kissinger is alive), and "Is my life a failure?" are, I claim, despite having a deceptively similar grammatical shape, very different kinds of questions. Evaluation of Caesar's life is subject to all the difficulties and ambiguities of imperfect knowledge, and one can disagree completely on the standards it would be appropriate to apply to his life, but this is just the usual run-of-the-mill uncertainty of all human judgment. Evaluation of someone still alive must also accommodate the possibility of change. In the modern world this would probably not take the form we saw in the case of the two Montefeltri, but one can't in principle exclude the possibility that Kissinger might suddenly follow the example of John Profumo and spend the rest of their lives working with the poor to rehabilitate themselves morally and atone for their reprehensible lives. "Is my life a failure?" has a different structure again. Only while it is still going on can I ask myself whether my life is a failure, because the dead ask no questions; while it is still going on, however, is an openended process, in which I am actively involved. Part of that involvement is making (individual or global) judgments about that life. I can try proleptically to "complete" it in imagination and judge the result, but the imaginative "completion" I impose may change at any moment, just as the standards of judgment may change, so any answer to the question is just the imaginative effervescence of a particular moment, a soap bubble sure to burst. When "my life" actually constitutes what is in any sense a "complete" object for judgment, I can't ask the question of success or failure because I am dead. Of course, human agents, individuals, and groups, can impose closure of context virtually *ad libitum,* and so no one can be prevented from choosing such a fixed "context" and an appropriate set of evaluative principles and declaring anything they want a "success" or a "failure." Adorno's American can simply decide that his life was a failure *because* of lack of economic success, and refuse to reopen the question at all; no one can prevent him from doing that. The idea, however, that many people have held is that there is one single, natural, all-encompassing context for a human life which *imposes itself;* it is in some strong sense "given" and not just chosen. This idea is one that is sometimes asserted, more often simply taken for granted, but has not, as far as I am aware, ever been argued for. If one does think about it, it seems an entirely ungrounded assumption. Perhaps reflecting on this question and possible answers to it can help one become clearer about the values one in fact holds, and even, in some marginal cases, about which ones one ought not to hold (even if one finds it hard or impossible actually to act on this). Conceivably, in some societies for some people (at some times) the question may be unavoidable, even if unanswerable. Certainly obsessive reflection on it is not a sign of particular profundity, but of psychic and social dysfunction. Nothing, then, suggests that the question itself has any answer in the sense in which it is intended.

To prevent misunderstanding, in conclusion, I am *not* claiming that one can never form a conception of one's own life as a whole or a single activity. Some people do this; some don't. However, even when someone does this, the way in which one's life will be construed as a unity will change over time. Young Ivan Ilyich will project his own life as pursuit of pleasure (sometimes) and (other times) as pursuit of social advancement; the older Ivan will think that both of these were mistaken. There is not one and only one construction that can be put on a human life. I am also not saying that there is *just* such a variable flow of different, changing constructions an individual puts on his or her life and that *all* of these are equally "good." Some are better than others—for instance, less self-deluded, less likely to cause pain to others, more likely to induce further human initiative, and so forth. These standards of saying what "good" amounts to also change and vary with circumstance. Some standards may show themselves to be (contextually) better than others *without* it being the case that there is only one canonical reading of my life as a single unified activity which inherently trumps all others, nor a clear set of goals, criteria, and standards which are in fact fixed or have unquestionable priority in evaluating a life as a success or a failure.

8

Metaphysics without Roots

In a photo showing Antonin Artaud just after his release from a mental institution (Figure 8.1), one can see on his face the traces of years of drug addiction, the malnourishment he suffered during the war, and the various "treatments" he was subject to, against his will, once they had removed him from the section for "incurables." The main treatments were "insulin therapy" and electroshock (fifty-eight sessions, in the course of one of which one of his vertebrae was fractured).

He is seated in three-quarter profile, gazing intently at an invisible point to his left, beyond the right-hand side of the picture frame. He covers his neck with the long, spindly fingers of his left hand, and, with his fingertips on his cheek and his thumb under his chin, he seems to be supporting the right half of his face. Or is he stroking his face? Or both? One mustn't say that this gesture is "ambiguous," because Artaud was convinced that gestures had a precise meaning and a logic of their own. A gesture, that is, is "ambiguous" only relative to a possible translation of it into words, but why would one even try to give such a translation, given that language, Artaud thinks, is itself a radically inadequate vehicle of meaning. "Tout vrai langage," he says, "serait incompréhensible."[1]

His head is so emaciated that in contrast his right ear seems disproportionately large, and his long, pointed nose, which turns down

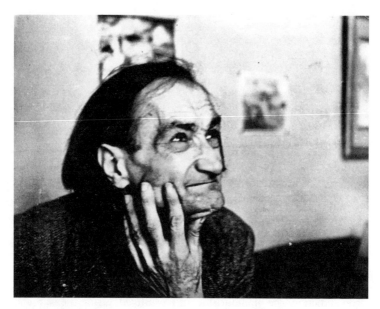

8.1 Antonin Artaud, 1947. Photograph by Georges Pastier

slightly like the beak of a toucan seems especially prominent. The face
has something of the bird of prey about it.

The grin of a malicious wise-ass child plays around his lips, and
the reason is that he is about to impart to us a revelation, to announce
to us something that will not at all please us: he has discovered a way
of abolishing the judgment of god. It was January 1948, and in the
studio of Radiodiffusion Française they were about to record on tape
the voice that no one who once has heard it can ever forget:

> J'ai appris hier
> (il faut croire que je retarde, ou peut-être n'est-ce qu'un faux
>   bruit, l'un de ces sales ragots comme il s'en colporte entre
>   évier et latrine à l'heure de la mise aux baquets des repas
>   une fois de plus ingurgités),
> J'ai appris hier[2]

Anyone with even a minimal knowledge of German literature would here immediately be reminded of the beginning of one of the oldest recorded works in a direct ancestor of the modern language, the *Hildebrandtslied* (eighth / ninth century?): "Ik gihorte dat seggen . . . ," but rather than following that train of thought, let's stay with a prosaic translation:

> I learned yesterday
> (Perhaps I was just slow or maybe it was a false rumour, one of
>   those filthy inventions one hears
> peddled between the kitchen sink and the latrine at the hour
>   when they put out the (once again) uneaten food into the
>   bins)
> I learned yesterday

The text of this projected radio broadcast, which has the title "To dispense with the judgment of god," was spoken by Artaud himself (with three friends of his who were actors) on tape. However, on the evening before the public broadcast was to take place, it was banned, ostensibly on the grounds that its contents were blasphemous and its mode of expression obscene. However, the tape recording still exists.[3]

What point was there in demanding the abolition of the judgment of god in 1948? The "judgment of god" was, as we all know, a legal institution which existed in the Dark Ages to bring about a decision in cases in which human reason failed and adequate proofs on either side were lacking. In cases like this, one "left the decision to god himself," as they said. However, the judgment of god hadn't been used as a technique for making legally binding decisions since, at the latest, the seventeenth century, so why should it need to be abolished in 1948? To be sure, one can use the term "judgment of god" to designate not just certain concrete old-Germanic legal procedures (ordeal by fire, duel, ordeal by water, and so forth), but also, in an eschatological sense, to refer to the Last Judgment. When Christian poets and thinkers, since antiquity, spoke about the Last Judgment, they seemed to produce a veritable phantasmagoria of particularly weird, bizarre, and macabre images and stories. So the Old High German poem usually called *Muspili* describes a duel at the end of days between the Antichrist and the prophet Elias. The prophet is wounded and the drops of his blood set the whole earth on fire:

[so da]z eliases pluot	in erda kitriufit,
[s]o inprinnant die perga,	poum ni kistentit
[e]hnihc in erdu	aha ar-truknent,
muor var[s]uuilhit sih	suilozot lougiu der himil,
mano uallit,	prinnit mittilagart. (ll. 50–54)

When the prophet Elias's blood drips down onto earth, the mountains begin to burn, not a single tree on earth remains upright, the rivers dry out, the moorland swallows itself up, the sky is carbonised in the heat, the moon falls—the whole inhabited earth burns.[4]

After this conflagration each human is called before the divine seat of judgment; no one can escape:

So denne der mahti-go	daz m[a]hal kipannit
khunninc	
dara scal queman	chunno ki-lihaz
denne ni kitar parno	den pan furi-sizzan
nohhein	
ni a[l]lero manno [u]elih	ze demo mahale sculi. (Z. ll. 31–34)

When this mighty king then proclaims an assembly, each clan must come. No one can miss the call to appear; there is no one among men who can fail to appear at this day of judgment.[5]

God in his capacity as the supreme judge ("der suanari, der mahti-go khunnic") then gives his verdict on each individual, and, in accordance with the Manicheaen orientation of western monotheism, this verdict always has the form of a strict dichotomy: salvation or damnation; bliss or perdition; the soul "goes to heaven" ("quemant . . . in himilo rihi," ll. 11–13) or to hell ("so verit si za uuize," l. 62). This explains the pious wish of all poor humans:

Inter oves locum presta
Et ab haedis me sequestra

Give me a place among your lambs
Keep me away from the goats[6]

God's judgment is always a clear "Yes" or "No": "Yes, you can join the flock of my sheep," or "No, off to hell with you." *Tertium non datur.* God's "judgment," to be sure, is, in the first instance, an action, not a sentence or proposition—God either really *takes* the person in question to himself or pushes him or her away. One can express these actions in sentences, if one so desires, but the very fact that God would use (human) language to formulate his judgment would already be a concession on his part to human weakness and finitude. He doesn't need to explain himself, certainly not in terms humans could comprehend.

Since these eschatological fantasies are not taken very seriously today either, one could still persist in wondering about the relevance of all this to us. In this regard too, the judgment of God would seem to be no more than a fading memory of a long-outgrown imaginative construct.

Christian conceptions, however, have had a longer historical reach in the West than this simple dismissal would suggest, and that is particularly true in this case. There is, namely, yet a further cosmological-theological turn that the judgment of God has taken which is of great and continuing philosophical significance: As the omnipotent creator of the world ("Cot allmahtigo / himil enti erda ga-uuoartahtos")[7] God takes care that every event and object in the universe is completely determinate in every aspect. Each event and object is specified down to the smallest possible detail of its composition, far beyond anything that we would even imagine in our wildest dreams.

This means that every star in the cosmos has an absolutely determinate temperature, even if this star is one we shall never have any awareness of. As a concomitant of this, in our own world, dichotomy reigns supreme. Every possible property *is* true of every object *or it is not true* of that object. Again, *tertium non datur.*

This idea gives rise to a traditional theological construction that connects, in a way that has seemed plausible to generations, three distinct thoughts. First, the space of pure possibilities has logical priority over reality. What is possible is there "first"; only a part of it is "realised" at any time. Second, that positivity has priority over negativity. Third, that it is spirit or mind—either the finite mind of humans or infinite divine spirit—that brings negation into the world. Two stones that simply lie next to each other, peacefully, in the desert, exist as the concrete realisation of one logical possibility; nothing more. Neither of them shows the slightest trace of "negation." It is only when the prospector arrives that he identifies the situation as one in which "gold is *not* there, because this stone is *not* gold."[8] If this is so, though, why assume that the principles of logic and reason have any kind of application to parts of reality that have not yet been, and perhaps never will be, investigated by humans? Here God jumps into the breach. He is there and has always been there; he created everything, after all. As an infinite and omnipotent spirit, God holds all things in his hands and takes care that the rules of logic retain their universal validity and that categories of reason can be applied to anything anywhere.

Artaud sees it differently. For him, reality is relative to the human body (not to mind or spirit) and is not to be conceived in the first instance as something positive, but through categories of negation. That is "real" which imposes itself so uncomfortably on my body that I cannot ignore it and also wish to swat it away. I can imagine that I am not in Cambridge, but rather sitting on a bench in the Parisian suburb of Ivry, or that Artaud and I, together, are in Rome, watching the execution of Béatrice Cenci. I can imagine anything you like, "whatever" (as Californians say); even things that are contradictory are possible "in thought." This is true until the body speaks and produces its pre-discursive cry "Ooow," a sound that is often, as it were, simply pressed out of my carcass:

> . . . ça veut
> SORTIR:
> la présence
> de ma douleur
> de corps

> . . . something wants
> TO EMERGE:
> The presence of the
> pain of my body[9]

The pain thus extruded from the body is a pre-linguistic "NO," and, as such, the germ of possible resistance to the world:

> C'est qu'on me pressait
> Jusqu'à mon corps
> Jusqu'au corps

> **Est c'est alors**
> **Que j'ai tout fait éclater**
> **Parce qu'à mon corps**
> **On ne touche jamais.**

> It is that one was harassing me
> Right to my body
> bodily

> **And then**
> **I made everything explode**
> **because my body**
> **no one shall ever touch.**

si fort qu'on me presse de questions
et que je nie toutes les questions
il y a un point
où je me trouve contraint
de dire non
   NON

No matter how much one has harassed me
With questions, and I have denied all those questions
There comes a point
When I feel compelled
To say no
   NO[10]

"Ooow" is not a statement or a proposition,[11] but the negation that takes place and vents itself in the sound "ooow" is the transcendental condition of the possibility of any statement or proposition whatever. It is something like a prelinguistic positing of the existence of the world. Suddenly something is there: a judgment can be made. So the body and its cussed orneriness is the ground of logic: without it there would be no "no" and hence no logic.[12]

Pain is not the only condition in which something is pressed out of the body, so that a physical negation becomes real and concrete. Shitting is also a process of negation: I do *not* wish to retain this matter any longer. (Therefore) *obviously* there exists some "thing" other than me: I want to extrude it. Obviously, too, I must exist, because I am trying to extrude / reject / negate it. So in addition to the principle "dolet mihi, ergo (aliquid) dolendum est, ergo est aliquid, ergo sum," there is now another that can be admitted: "caco, ergo est (aliquid) cacandum, ergo est aliquid, ergo sum."[13]

That god never shits is a proof that he does not exist.

Dieu, est-il un être?
S'il en est un c'est de la merde.

S'il n'en est pas un
il n'est pas
Or il n'est pas

Is god an entity?
If so, he is made of shit
If he is not,
He doesn't exist.
Ergo he does not exist.[14]

No amount of complicated theological fancy footwork can get around this set of evident facts. "Negative" theology emphasises the utter transcendence of god and is therefore comfortable with the claim that *in the ordinary human sense* "god" does not exist: he "is" something special and "beyond being," certainly not an individual "entity" or a "thing," like a building or a hamster, nor, of course, is he an abstract property like "blueness" or "warmth." However, one can actually turn the arguments of the negative theologians around: How could something which is not in any sense an "entity," that is, which is a nothing, be worthy of veneration or adoration? More importantly, how could an absolute non-thing sit in judgment over humans? If god is a no-thing that absolutely negates (and nothing else), how can one call that unconditional and undifferentiated negation a "*judgment*?" That "*everything* that comes to be" also deserves to perish,[15] is a devastating judgment, but it is not an "absolute" judgment. Rather it is a distinctly limited and conditional one, because it refers only to "everything that comes to be." The decision which was embodied in the judgment of god, however—god's thumbs-up or thumbs-down—was not supposed to be a form of absolute negation: it was supposed to distinguish between sheep and goats, not condemn them both equally and without possible mitigation or qualification. Even if, in point of fact, there happen not to be any sheep because all humans are sinners, that is still a separate matter. To abolish the very possibility of a positive outcome (as one would if god was just a principle of absolute negation) would make the notion of a divine *judgment* meaningless.

A god like that, an absolutely empty process absolutely negating everything, would be, as Artaud says, like the march of a limitless army of crab lice:

> [Dieu est]
> ... comme le vide qui avance avec toutes ses formes
> dont la représentation la plus parfaite
> est la marche d'un groupe incalculable de morpions.[16]

> [God is]
> ... like the emptiness which advances with all his
>   forms
> the most perfect representation of which
> is the march of an unsurveyable troupe of crab lice.

The arsehole, one might say, is the measure of reality *par excellence* for Artaud, because the world itself is terribly shitty and it is also an instrument of cognition, because, although I can fart out any possibilities I wish, the arsehole will, under normal circumstances, be able to distinguish between empty and full loads. Seen from the point of view of traditional metaphysics: no shit without farts; but for Artaud, without reality (that is matter that is negated by the body itself) no possibilities:

> Alors
> L'espace de la possibilité
> Me fut un jour donné
> Comme un grand pet
> Que je ferai.

> Thus,
> The space of possibilities

Was given to me one day
Like a huge fart
That I shall let out.

If there is no divine tribunal, then there is no heaven and no hell, no absolute Up or Down, Above or Below. Poor Lenz, in Büchner's story,[17] can still be sorry that he cannot march on his head, and we can continue to have pity for him, but Celan's remark that " for someone who is walking on his head, heaven is an abyss"[18] has lost its moorings. In a world without hierarchically structured verticality, even "revolution" has a completely different meaning than we would normally take it to have. Maybe it would be a reversal of direction in a horizontal plane:

L'homme est malade parce qu'il est mal construit.
Il faut se décider à le mettre à nu pour lui gratter cet
    animalcule qui le démange mortellement,
    dieu
[. . .]
Lorsque vous lui aurez fait un corps sans organes, alors que
    vous l'aurez délivré de
tous ses automatismes et rendu sa véritable liberté.

Alors vous lui réapprendrez à danser à l'envers
Comme dans le délire des bals musette
Et cet envers sera son véritable endroit.

Man is ill because he has been badly constructed
We have to strip him naked in order to scratch
    that tiny animal that is itching him to death
    god

. . . .
When you have made him a body without organs,

Then you will have delivered him from all his automatisms
And have given him his true freedom.

Then you will teach him again to dance backwards
As if in the delirium of a dance in a cheap café
And this "backwards" will be his true place.

In a dance, too, there is no Above and Below, just Forward and Backward; perhaps there is a temporal order—*this* step before *that*
step—and a direction, but no hierarchy. Like a well-constructed car,
a skilled dancer has, as it were, a forward gear and a reverse, and he
or she can, and must, of course, steer. Dancers do not simply let themselves drift in a passive or contemplative way in the way described in
Hölderlin's "Mnemosyne":

> Und immer ins Ungebundene
> Gehet eine Sehnsucht. Vieles ist aber
> Zu behalten. Und Noth die Treue.
> Vorwärts aber und rückwärts
> Wollen wir nicht sehen
> Uns wiegen lassen
> Wie auf schwankem Kahne der See

> And always
> There is a yearning that seeks the unbound. But much
> Must be retained. And loyalty is needed.
> Forward, however, and back we will
> Not look. Be lulled and rocked as
> On a awaying skiff of the sea[19]

But why should loyalty or fidelity (*Treue*) be necessary (*Noth*)? Why
not resist the longing to plunge into that which is unbound (*das
Ungebundene*)?

So neither Lenz, nor Hölderlin. But the direction is undoubtedly backwards; how far back? It is no surprise that Artaud rejects the world of modern technology, but what is interesting is his interpretation of what it is he is rejecting. Even in 1947–1948 he was able to see the modern technical world as climaxing in the biotechnological manipulation of human beings. He ascribes to Americans and Russians—in his view the two most technology technology-obsessed modern populations—a theology which combines in equal parts atomic energy, biotechnology, and an insect-like hypocrisy:

> . . . ce qu'on a appelé les microbes
> c'est dieu,
> et savez-vous avec quoi les Américains et les Russes font leurs
>   atomes?
> Il les font avec les microbes de Dieu.[20]

> . . . what one has called microbes
> is god,
> and do you know with what the Americans and Russians
>   make their atoms?
> They make them with the microbes of god.

The "sick and badly constructed human" must be completely rebuilt. For this reason, one must take seriously the American experiments with artificial insemination which are treated so ironically at the beginning of Artaud's text. These experiments are the natural expression of the life of a population that will do literally anything to avoid a direct encounter with the basic facts of life. Any population that wants to inseminate without intercourse, that makes war with such a huge apparatus of machines, in order to avoid even the slightest possible danger, and which looks for its satisfactions in various forms of pseudo-intoxication, clearly knows nothing about the fire of immediate experience, and the way in which it can give one access to reality. Poverty of experience, however, brings with it, eventually, a loss of reality.

Isn't the above, one might ask, nothing but a trotting out of old hats and coats from the huge wardrobe of European reactionary thought, articles of clothing that never had much shape or elegance, and are not looking distinctly shoddy and threadbare? Didn't Heidegger say much the same thing as Artaud, to be sure in a way perhaps less lyrical, in 1935?

> This Europe, in its catastrophic and deluded way, always about to stab itself in the back, lies today in the pincers of Russia, on the one side, and America, on the other. Russia and America are, from a metaphysical point of view, the same thing: [they both instantiate] the same frenzy of unleashed technology and rootless organisation of normed human beings.[21]

We do know, in the case of Heidegger, what he imagined to be the opposite of "rootless organisation," because we can read the entry he made in the *Deutsches Führerlexikon* (1934 / 1935): "Heidegger, Martin . . . springs from an old allemannic-swabian peasant clan, which, on the material side (Kempf) can be traced as working the same farm as far back as 1510."[22] So are hunters and gatherers, who, of necesssity, would have no knowledge of any such form of persistent agricultural property, necessarily rootless, and "forgetful of Being?"

Artaud will have no truck either with the belligerent ideal American, produced hygienically by artificial insemination, nor with the sentimentalised south German peasant-idyll of a Heidegger. He wants neither to be a "shepherd of Being" (as Heidegger would have it) nor its automatic answering-machine:

> j'aime mieux le peuple qui mange à même la terre le délire
>   d'où il est né,
> je parle des Tarahumaras

mangeant le Peyotls à même le sol
pendant qu'il naît[23]

I prefer [to the Americans]
that population which eats its delirium straight from the
    ground from which
    it was born
I'm speaking of the Tarahumaras
who eat peyotl right off the ground
while it is growing

People who crouch on the ground to eat their peyotl are certainly no less connected with the "aboriginal powers" of the universe than swabian peasants are. Nomadic life in constant movement is not, as Heidegger would have it, necessarily a life of superficiality. Nor is it clear what metaphysical objection Heidegger could have to a life conducted "backwards" (*à l'envers*), or to a life of delirium. The abolition of the judgment of god is not an "overcoming of metaphysics." Artaud is an atheist and an anti-theologian, but, in contrast to many analytic and Continental philosophers, he is not afraid of "metaphysics." In fact, he even describes his project in "Pour en finir avec le jugement de dieu" as the search for a language, capable of articulating "the highest metaphysical truths" ("les verities métaphysiques les plus élevées").[24] Nevertheless his text does not end with the enunciation of some truth about "the essence of man," but with a highly conditional prediction, the expression of a hope: Since there is no judgment of god, man has no true place in the world, but if his poor construction can be remedied, the backward position in a constantly changing, delirious world can become "my place."

9

Context

In March 1954 my grandmother, with whom I, seven years old at the time, was living during one of my father's periodic sojourns in the hospital, bought a television set, the first I had ever seen. It had a small round screen, not a rectangular one of the kind that has since become most common, so that looking at it was rather like peering through a porthole. The screen was about twenty centimeters in diameter, and the image was, of course, in black and white. It was, however, a fascinating apparatus, attracting the neighbours occasionally to watch a programme. One of the first programmes I remember watching was the so-called Army-McCarthy Hearings of a subcommittee of the US Senate which were broadcast live in the afternoons—this, at least, is how I remember it. That most of what was happening on the screen was not fully comprehensible to me should come as no surprise. I had virtually none of the background information that would have been required to make sense of the exceedingly complex events that were taking place. As I now realise, the United States at that time was going through one of its periodic exercises in paranoid hysteria, and this was centred on a US Senator named Joe McCarthy, who whipped up as much hatred and suspicion as he could, hoping to use a particularly crude version of anti-Communism as an instrument for his own political advancement. His specific tactic was to try to intimidate various institutions, such as the film studios of Hollywood, by issuing wild and completely unsupported accusations that their loyalty to the United States was compromised because of the large number of Communist sympathisers who filled their senior positions. He had some success initially against politicians, celebrities, and people in the media, but he made the mistake of trying to use the same tactics against the US Army. It turned out that that institution was fully capable of defending itself robustly against completely fabricated charges, and in the televised hearings he initiated against the US Army, McCarthy was himself shown up for what he was and discredited. The drama of the spectacle was only too apparent, even to a child like me, although it was very hard to keep track of all the people involved in the convoluted forensic ballet that was played out on the television each afternoon. McCarthy was visibly a bully of a type with which I was only all too familiar in school and in everyday life, but, oddly enough, for reasons that were not clear to me, he did not seem to be getting his way, as such people usually, in my experience, did. The resistance he encountered was to me puzzling.

The particular part of the McCarthy-Army proceedings, however, which made the deepest impression on me was the use of a certain photograph. McCarthy showed the other Senators and the members of the audience a huge blow-up of a photograph showing a young man standing in front of what seemed to be the fuselage of an airplane and shaking the hand of an older man. The young man was a private, the lowest rank of soldier, and the older man was the Secretary of the Army. What was the Secretary of the Army doing on an airfield meeting a private? The image was technically absolutely clear and perfect, and McCarthy explained to everyone involved what one could see in the picture. There seemed to be no doubt but that the photo was genuine—no one denied that, or claimed that the photo was forged or staged—there also seemed to be consensus about the identities of the two people shown and, indeed, about what the picture "meant." The next day, however, McCarthy's opponents showed that the same picture which McCarthy had exhibited the day before was actually a detail of a larger photo: McCarthy's picture had been cropped to exclude another person, a third figure, standing with the young man and the older man. This changed the meaning of the photo, as everyone again seemed to agree, turning it into exactly the opposite of that which McCarthy had given it.

This was not, as McCarthy had claimed, some kind of secret and potentially subversive meeting between the Secretary of the Army and a spy, but a public event, and the private just happened to be the first in a whole queue of people waiting to greet the Secretary. The new more complete uncropped picture also contained in its left corner the image of the coat of a yet further *fourth* man standing in front of the fuselage of this airplane. If one had been able to see clearly who the fourth man was, this, I recall imagining, might have given the picture yet a different meaning. I remember very vividly sitting in my grandmother's upstairs sitting room, where the television set was placed, and realising that the meaning of the photograph—whatever it was—depended almost entirely on the context and the way it was framed. I recall phantasising that every day henceforth they would continue to reveal that the photos shown on the previous days were just isolated segments, to be supplemented in the days to come, where each addition changed the meaning of what had gone before, *and that this process could continue without stopping indefinitely.* I also recall thinking that as the photos became bigger and bigger, detail would be lost: If the photo was of the whole airfield rather than of what was happening in front of this airplane, how could one recognise who was who? If the photo had been of the whole world, even the airfield would have been invisible. Loss of detail also meant loss of meaning. Similarly, if one focused more and more on one tiny detail, blowing it up more and more, the meaning would also be lost. In retrospect, I can now see that this line of thought was confused because I was conflating two different things: the cropping of an existing photo and taking a photo in a particular format.

The proper conclusion for a theist (in particular a Platonistically inclined theist) to draw would have been that "eventually" there was a final definitive image, in the mind of God, which would *include* (in some way) all the details of all previous smaller pictures, even though the pictures could get infinitely smaller and smaller. At that point, in God's mind, the dance of the billions of veils would in principle stop, would have to stop, even if for various reasons, for instance, the limitation of our human powers, we could never actually see or encompass this final image. Even at the age of seven, however, I found myself incapable of drawing this conclusion; it seemed to me self-evident that the process could continue *ad libitum* with a continually shifting context and constantly changing meaning. There was no endpoint, not even an imaginary one, although at some point there might be a loss of any ability to focus. The conception was incoherent.

I am inclined, in retrospect, to see in this early experience the germs of some views that have continued to seem to me to be of central importance. First, meaning (and consequently knowledge) is essentially contextual; second, meaning must be a collective, that is a social phenomenon; third, there is no final all-encompassing framework which puts everything together; finally, the absence of such a framework, and thus of any "final" meaning visibly does not entirely destroy the phenomenon of local meaning. If these views are at all correct, it would seem that asking questions about meaning, success, life as a whole, or one's real self, require rather a different approach from any of those discussed in this book. The task becomes not one of looking for some single thing, but managing, as Nietzsche suggests, (sometimes) multiple shifting perspectives, and negotiating smooth transitions—transitions that are "as smooth as possible" (whatever that means)—between irreducibly different contexts.

If one wants to call this a "world view," then I have no objection to that.

Notes

Preface

1. K. Gödel, "Über formal unentscheidbare Sätze der *Principia mathematica* und verwandter Systeme," *Monatshefte für Mathematik und Physik,* December 1931, pp. 173–198.

2. This was clearly an obsession of Foucault's at least during certain periods. Compare his *Surveiller et punir* (Gallimard, 1975).

3. G. W. F. Hegel, *Grundlinien der Philosophie des Rechts,* in *Werke in zwanzig Bänden,* ed. Eva Moldenhauer and Karl Markus Michel (Suhrkamp, 1970), vol. 7, pp. 11–28.

4. See Charles Péguy, *Victor-Marie, comte Hugo* in *Oeuvres* (Pléïade, 1992), vol. 3, pp. 331–332.

5. Gottfried Leibniz, *de arte characteristica,* in C. I. Gerhardt, *Die philosophischen Schriften von Gottfried Wilhelm Leibniz* (Weidmann, 1890), vol. 7, p. 125.

6. G. F. W. Hegel, *Die Phänomenologie des Geistes,* in *Werke in zwanzig Bänden,* ed. Eva Moldenhauer and Karl Markus Michel (Suhrkamp, 1970), vol. 3, (B) 4.B.

7. Berthold Brecht, *"Das Leben des Galilei"* 13. Bild.

8. Karl Marx, *Kritik des Gothaer Programms,* in *Marx-Engels Werke* (hereafter *MEW*) 19 (Dietz, 1962), p. 32.

9. This strand of Nietzschean thought is developed most fully in T. W. Adorno and Max Horkheimer, *Die Dialektik der Aufklärung* (Fischer, 1969).

1. Who Needs a World View?

1. L. Althusser, *Lénine et la philosophie* (Maspero, 1969).

2. Other striking examples would include: the worldview of Roman imperialism (*Tu Romane, memento* Aeneid Book VI). Even Kantianism can be construed as interpellating me in this way: "Hey, you, rational agent (and potential member of a Kingdom of Ends) there," and to that extent it, too, can be considered to be a world view. The mechanism at work here is made very explicit in Judaism. In the *seder,* the ritual dinner at Passover, certain stories are told about Moses, the Pharoah, and the departure of the children of Israel from Egypt. However, in most versions of the ceremony one is also told how to interpret these stories as relevant. The worst possible reaction to these stories is: "This is what happened *to the Jews of old.*" To have this reaction is to accept the historical validity of the narratives, but distance oneself from their interpellative function, to say "That doesn't affect *me.*" To say this is the worst reaction is to emphasise how important for the world view that the persons addressed adopt the identity thus thrust on them.

3. A. MacIntyre, *After Virtue,* 3rd ed. (Duckworth, 2007).

4. Krigler will have known about the "scientific world view" (*wissenschaftliche Weltauffassung*) propagated by some in the Vienna Circle; see *Wissenschaftliche Weltauffassung: Der Wiener Kreis,* in *Veröffentlichungen des Vereins Ernst Mach* (Wien: Wolf Verlag, 1929); but it did not play much of a role in his thinking. Perhaps he thought it was just a contribution to an academic quarrel or perhaps he thought it too limited in its scope. In contrast, Daniel Bell's "end of ideology" (Bell, *The End of Ideology: On the Exhaustion of Political Ideas in the Fifties* [Free Press, 1960]) was an attempt to move the Democratic Party in the United States further away from various left-wing projects rather than a serious contribution to the understanding of anything. The reader will note that I do not distinguish in this work between world view and ideology, or between *Weltbild* and *Weltanschauung.* I try to say something about the concept of "ideology" in my *The Idea of a Critical Theory* (Cambridge University Press, 1981, chapter 1).

5. This was just before the period (1965) when Sartre said in a radio interview that "*Tout anticommuniste est un chien.*"

6. Later I saw that this is a version of what came to be called "the Whig view" of history (see Herbert Butterfield, *The Whig Interpretation of History*

[G. Bell and Sons, 1931]), although Krigler, of course, had never heard of that and did not use this term for it.

7. See my "Thucydides, Nietzsche and Williams," in *Outside Ethics* (Princeton University Press, 2005), and "Nietzsche's Ethnology," *Arion* 24, no. 3 (Winter 2017), pp. 89–116.

8. One of the purported "founding moments" of the democracy was a series of reforms instituted by Kleisthenes at the very end of the sixth century BC. See the essay by John Dunn on ancient democracy in his *Democracy: A History* (Atlantic Monthly Press, 2006).

9. Connoisseurs will see Heidegger in the background here.

10. As I gradually came to realise when I subscribed to and began to read articles in the journal Krigler particularly recommended to me, *Wissenschaft und Weltbild,* this was a way of looking at things that was not completely original to him either, although he propounded it with inimitable intellectual verve; rather it fit in very neatly with the sorts of discussions that were taking place in Vienna, where Krigler had studied for a short time just after leaving Hungary.

11. For example, in periodicals like *Time* magazine (for which Krigler had a burning and visceral loathing). He would repeat what was a kind of mantra for him: "Unless your knowledge surpasses that of the *Time* magazine, you shall not enter into the Kingdom of God." He never really mastered the use of articles in English. (Then he would apologise and explain why, despite this, he was definitely *not* a gnostic.) The boarding school was a completely self-contained "total institution" located in the buildings of an old sanatorium with extensive grounds: it might just as well have been in Csongrad, where Krigler had grown up. Students were forbidden to leave the grounds, and the nearest shop was in any case several miles away; no radio, newspapers, or magazines were permitted, so I had never seen a copy of *Time.* Krigler's references to it, though, had built up in my mind an image of a publication that was dangerous and addictive and, by an association of ideas natural to an adolescent in a Catholic boarding school, probably very sexy: a kind of combination of *The Communist Manifesto* and *Playboy.* How great was my disappointment when after my arrival at university in New York in 1963 I found *Time* to be so plodding, so exceptionally badly written and so ill-informed as to discourage perusal by any non-masochist. Krigler also had an obsession (this time positive) with Heidegger's *Holzwege,* so one of the

first things I did upon arriving in New York was to go to Adler's German Bookshop (which was on Fifth Avenue at about Twenty-First Street) and procure a copy; it turned out to be very much what I had expected it to be.

12. So Heidegger (*Brief über den Humanismus,* in *Platons Lehre von der Wahrheit* [Francke, 1949]), not Jacques Maritain.

13. J. S. Mill thought history was about the choice between liberalism and despotism (at best enlightened and benign ["Asoka"] or malevolent).

14. Lenin, *State and Revolution* (various editions); Trotsky, "*Their Morals and Ours*" (Pathfinder Press, 1973).

15. Krigler was keen on books like Vance Packard's *The Hidden Persuaders* (1957), which describe the deleterious effects of the culture of advertising. The books he read and recommended seem very out of date today, but more recent history gives us no reason to think that things have got any better in this respect. He adopted the principle of never buying anything he had seen advertised. In fairness, it was less difficult for a member of a religious order who wore a cassock and ate at the common table to do this in 1959 than it would be for many people in 2018. Krigler was also fully aware that this decision of his was nothing but a gesture; however, he saw that as no objection to it.

16. This was from Nietzsche, of course.

17. "Picking and choosing," that is, simply taking something at random and making some kind of informed choice based on an existing preference, was the topic of one of Sidney Morgenbesser's few papers: "Picking and Choosing," Edna Ullmann-Margalit and Sidney Morgenbesser, in *Social Research* 4, no. 4 (Winter 1977), pp. 757–785.

18. Marx, "... *der Reichtum der Gesellschaften, in welchen kapitalistische Produktionsweise herrscht, erscheint als eine 'ungeheure Warensammlung,' die einzelne Ware als seine Elementarform*" (beginning of *Das Kapital,* vol. 1).

19. Many members of the Tory Party are keen to introduce "choice" into the areas of medicine and health provision (and education). However, when my leg is broken, I don't want "choice of doctors" or "choice of treatment." I'm not qualified to judge and if I am in pain the last thing I want to do is make decisions. What I want is for my leg to be competently set (and to be sure that competent treatment is universally available to me and others who need it for free). Similarly, ex hypothesi, those who have not finished their education cannot be "informed and competent consumers." If they were "in-

formed and competent" they wouldn't be at school. That's one of the points of education—that you are to emerge from it a radically changed person, capable of experiences that were inaccessible to you and of making judgments that would have been beyond you before.

20. In the novel it is the young Russian woman Claudia Chauchat, who is described as pronouncing the German word "*menschlich*" as "*määhnschlich*," but this was Krigler's slightly magyarised pronunciation of the word, too. During my trawls through German literature I had also for some reason never run across Goethe's "*Wanderers Sturmlied*," but when I first read it in 1963, I immediately thought of Krigler, who was in many ways a kind of archaic peasant type, as "der kleine, schwarze, feurige Bauer."

21. John Dewey, *Reconstruction in Philosophy* (Cosimo Classics, 2008); see also his *Logic: The Theory of Enquiry* (Holt, 1938); *The Quest for Certainty*, in *John Dewey: The Late Works*, vol. 4, ed. Jo Ann Boydston (Southern Illinois University Press, 1988); and *Human Nature and Conduct* (Modern Library, 1922).

22. Ernest Nagel, *Gödel's Proof*, rev. ed. (New York University Press, 2001); Tarski, "The Semantic Conception of Truth," in *Readings in Philosophic Analysis*, ed. H. Feigl and W. Sellars (Appleton-Century-Crofts, 1949), pp. 51–85.

23. Martin Heidegger, *Holzwege* (Frankfurt: Klostermann, 1963), pp. 69–104.

24. Béla actually took what came later to be called the "Maoist" reading of the dialectic: *all* human societies, not only class societies, were constructed around contradictions. We don't, however, know what form the antagonistic contradictions of a classless society will take, and a fortiori we know nothing about how they might be overcome. He was keen on the "materialism" of Communism, although, as he emphasised, "matter / material" did not mean the same thing as what we now called "matter" (any more than for Thales "water" was the stuff that floated in the Aegean), but was a deeply active metaphysical principle. So perhaps, he speculated, the dialectic would shift so that it did not primarily express itself in the internal structure of human society, but in the relation between humanity as a whole and nature as a whole.

25. The priests at my school had little difficulty with the Protestant doctrine of "justification by faith alone" (*sola fidei*), although they did

occasionally, and mischievously, point out that even St. Paul, the inventor
and patron saint of this doctrine, also said in a much cited passage that love
was more important than faith (*2 Corinthians*), and, of course, not even
Protestants would deny that true faith would express itself in action. On the
other hand, they were scathing about that other pillar of the Reformation,
the fetishistic focus on scripture alone (*sola scriptura*). First of all, the idea
that scripture will reveal its meaning in principle to any believer, more or less
without mediation was, if taken strictly, deeply unphilological. Texts do not,
contra what Lutherans seem to think, interpret themselves. No text makes
any sense at all except relative to the traditional practices of a community
of interpreters, who collated the texts, wrote the grammars, and put together
the lexica which I use, so even at this level the priority of the community
over the individual is clear. Furthermore, even a very cursory knowledge of
the history of the early church was needed to see that the canon of what
counted as scripture didn't get established until the second and third centuries (even if some of the texts were around in some form or another before that time). What went into the canon was decided on in a long historical process. So rather than the church being founded on scripture, it was
actually the other way around. Even if one dates the composition of some
of the very earliest documents in the canon to the 50s of the first century,
that is still a full two decades after the establishment of the church (in some
form or other). The Gospel of John thus has standing because the church
accepted it at some point as one of a group of aides-mémoires which were
useful because they expressed *what the church could recognise as its own doctrines*. So, when the Lutheran intoned with great pathos "*DAS WORT* sie
sollen lassen stan" ["They should leave The Word alone"], Rabelais (and
Erasmus and Montaigne) might be inclined to retort: "*Which* word exactly,
and how interpreted?" If one really thought that God was omnipotent, then
it would not be beyond his powers to endow a highly idiosyncratic and con-
tingently collected set of historical documents with great authority, but
then it would not be beyond his power also to inspire each Pope, regardless
of the contingencies of his life, directly whenever he was speaking *ex ca-
thedra*. This is why the Protestant thumping his Bible can so easily look to
Catholics like a witch doctor brandishing his fetish. The witch doctor has a
small stone or a crude wooden sculpture with feathers and studded with
nails. He doesn't necessarily actually know what the statue is, what god it

represents or what it means, but that isn't important. He attributes to this piece of wood great spiritual meaning and imaginary powers; it is powerful medicine. Similarly, the Lutheran treats his Bible and the words in it as something onto which he projects some great significance which the words themselves certainly do not have. Compared to this, the Consecration in a Catholic Mass is merely an especially highly charged form of speech act.

26. William James, "The Will to Believe," in *The Will to Believe & Other Essays in Popular Philosophy* (Longmans, 1897); L. Feuerbach, "Das Wesen des Christentums," in *Werke in sechs Bänden,* ed. Erich Thies (Suhrkamp, 1971), vol. 5; Marx, *Kritik der Hegelschen Rechtsphilosophie,* in *MEW* (Dietz, 1960), vol. 1.

27. Father Krigler used also to make a similar point, citing the (failed) sub-Feuerbachian attempts by one of the Communist regimes to reconfigure "Christmas" (once it had been decided that it could not simply be abolished) as "Festival of Bread."

28. Compare the discussion about the use of authentic instruments in early music. It has been pointed out that certain keyboard instruments which *sounded* exceptionally loud to musicians and audiences when they were originally introduced, sound weak and thin to us, because we are comparing them with the sound of a modern concert piano. So using authentic instruments will have the reverse of the intended effect. As has been pointed out, what we would really need, if one follows the line of argument out, is not just authentic instruments, but also ears unaffected by the intervening history of instruments and of music. But how does one "unhear" the Bechstein piano or *Tristan*?

29. James, "The Will to Believe."

30. C. S. Peirce, "How to Make Our Ideas Clear," *Popular Science Monthly* 12 (January 1878), pp. 286–302.

31. William James, "What Pragmatism Means" (reprinted in various collections of James's papers, e.g., *Pragmatism,* ed. Burkardt, Bowers, & Skrupskelis [Harvard University Press, 1907]).

32. Arthur Schopenhauer, *Die Welt als Wille und Vorstellung* (Diogenes, 2017).

33. Nietzsche, *Die Geburt der Tragödie,* in *Sämtliche Werke: Kritische Studien-Ausgabe,* ed. Giorgio Colli and Mazzino Montinari (de Gruyter, 1980), vol. 1.

34. Sidney on Gary Becker: "If you run into him on the street, you never know if he'll say hello to you. You know, he first has to calculate the cost of lost opportunities." He also told a story about meeting Luce, the coauthor of a standard work on rational decision theory, who had just been offered a job at another university and was worrying about what to do. He reported that he said to Luce: "Luce, you're one of the world's great experts on rational decision theory. Don't worry, use rational decision theory to help you make up your mind." To which Luce is said to have replied to him: "Sidney, this is serious." Another instance, perhaps, of something that was true but didn't work. Especially charismatic individuals become magnets for anecdotes, and Sidney was no exception. I don't believe he was the person who originally coined the other well-known *bon mot* about Becker: "His wife kills herself; he writes a book on the rationality of suicide." This does not seem to me in Sidney's style and I never heard him say this. I suspect it has its origin elsewhere and came to be assigned to him by attraction.

35. *Spiegel* interview with Heidegger, published, at Heidegger's own request, only after his death (May 1976).

36. Nietzsche, *Zur Genealogie der Moral,* in *Sämtliche Werke: Kritische Studien-Ausgabe,* ed. Giorgio Colli and Mazzino Montinari (de Gruyter, 1980), vol. 5.

37. Hegel, *Die Phänomenologie des Geistes,* in *Werke in zwanzig Bänden,* ed. Eva Moldenhauer and Karl Markus Michel (Suhrkamp, 1970), vol. 3, B. IV; L. Trotsky, *Literature and Revolution* (International Publishers, 1925).

38. Goethe, *Zahme Xenien IX:* "Wer Wissenschaft und Kunst besitzt, hat auch Religion;/wer jene beiden nicht besitzt, der habe Religion" ["He who has knowledge and art, also has religion;/he who has neither of these, let him get religion"].

39. Friedrich Schiller in his famous essay "Über Anmut und Würde" (numerous editions).

40. "Saviour" (σωτήρ) was a word widely used in inscriptions to refer to someone who gave any kind of help, including rich people who helped out in time of famine ("eueregetisme," see Paul Veyne, *Le pain et le cirque* [Seuil, 1976]) or emperors who granted municipal privileges, so calling Jesus "saviour" did not actually in itself mean much, and there seem to have been a variety of views, most of which only very gradually came to be sorted out as deviant and unacceptable ("heretical" in the later terminology).

41. G. W. F. Hegel, *Grundlinien der Philosophie des Rechts,* in *Werke in zwanzig Bänden,* ed. Eva Moldenhauer and Karl Markus Michel (Suhrkamp, 1970), vol. 7, p. 28.

42. *Platonis apologia socratis.*

2. Games and Proverbs

1. Cf. Edward Snow, *Inside Bruegel: The Play of Images in Children's Games* (North Point Press, 1997).

2. W. H. Auden, "Musée des Beaux Arts," 1938.

3. I'm grateful to Tom Stern for putting some of the points in this paragraph to me very vividly in discussion. The demand for a reflexive turn was an essential constituent of the Critical Theory of the Frankfurt School.

4. K. Marx, *Die deutsche Ideologie,* in *MEW* (Dietz, 1958), vol. 3, p. 425f.

5. Plutarch, *Vita,* 8.

6. G. Lessing, *Laoköon* in *Werkausgabe* (Bibiographisches Institut, 1911), vol. 4.

7. At the Old Bailey in London, 1878.

8. This point is made by Proust about successive hearings of a piece of music (*À l'ombre des jeunes filles en fleur* [Gallimard, 110]).

9. Related thoughts are to be found in F. Guatarri and G. Deleuze, *L'Anti-Oedipe* (Minuit, 1972).

3. Enlightenment, Genealogy, and the Historicality of Concepts

1. T. W. Adorno and Max Horkheimer, *Die Dialektik der Aufklärung* (Fischer, 1969).

2. Michel Foucault in *Dits et écrits,* ed. D. Defert and F. Ewald (Gallimard, 1994), pp. 562–578.

3. Foucault, *Dits et écrits.*

4. Gadamer, *Wahrheit und Methode* (Niemeyer, 1960).

5. "History will absolve me," Fidel Castro is reported to have said to his trial for insurrection in October 1953.

6. Adorno et al., *The Authoritarian Personality* (Harper, 1950).

7. Frede and Burnyeat, *The Original Sceptics* (Hackett, 1997).

8. Of course, in another sense, to use a conditional implies that there is some necessity or at any rate some lawlike connection between events. Thus, to say "If I had dropped it, it would have broken" makes sense only if (a) I envisage the possibility that I did not drop it, but also (b) I assume that things dropped always (or, generally?) break.

9. If a characteristic nineteenth-century philosophical fear is "determinism"—that I am not "free" even in my smallest actions—the characteristic ancient fear was "fatalism"—that despite my ability to do in any individual case whatever I liked, the final *result* would turn out to be beyond my control.

10. Herbert Butterfield, *The Whig Interpretation of History* (Norton, 1965).

11. Aristotle, *Metaphysics,* Book A.

12. Marx, *Das Elend der Philosophie,* in *MEW* (Dietz, 1960), vol. 4.

13. A method is a way of proceeding. If one thinks about it, one would have to distinguish a number of different kinds of "methods" associated with science.

First, there might be a "method of enquiry (or discovery)," that is a specification of steps one could take when trying to find something out in order to maximise the chances of success. A "method" need not, of course, be a "recipe," which is rather a set of steps that virtually ensure success, if correctly followed. As many have pointed out, there is no "sure way" to success in enquiry, but this does not mean there might not be pointers that were useful, at least, in preventing the pursuit of obvious dead ends.

Second, there might be a "method of justification," that is, a specification of the ways in which I might try to support claims I make that I have discovered something, such as a new law or new regularity. Third, what one might call the "method of representation," that is, of expounding and displaying my results (*Darstellungsmethode*). There might in fact be more than one useful way of displaying my results, depending on my purpose. In particular, I might think that different methods were appropriate for an expert audience or in a paedagogical context.

For "*Darstellungemethode*" one can see Marx, *Grundrisse der Kritik der politischen Ökonomie* (Dietz, 1974), pp. 21ff.

14. Aristotle, *Ethica Nichomachea,* 1134b.

15. Edward Craig, *Knowledge and the State of Nature* (Oxford University Press, 1990); B. Williams, *Truth and Truthfulness* (Princeton University Press, 2002).

16. Nietzsche, *Sämtliche Werke: Kritische Studienausgabe in 15 Bänden,* ed. Giorgio Colli and Mazzino Montinari (De Gruyter, 1980), vol. 5.

4. Life Is a Game

1. Wittgenstein rightly reminds us that that not all "games" have rules—the child who throws a ball against a wall may be said to be playing a game for which there are no rules. So games with rules, goals, scores, and a notion of winning and losing constitute only one class of "games," but let us ignore this qualification, as those who try to imagine social interaction as based on rules generally do.

2. Reprinted in Clifford Geertz's *The Interpretation of Cultures* (Basic Books, 1973).

3. Aristotle, *Ethica Nichomachea*, 1100a ff.

4. Onoda Hiro, the last Japanese combatant of World War II, surrendered in the Philippines in 1974.

5. The Metaphysical Need and the Utopian Impulse

1. Benedict Anderson, *Imagined Communities* (Verso, 1983). See also Eric Hobsbawm and Terence Ranger, eds., *The Invention of Tradition* (Cambridge University Press, 1983).

2. I realise that this notion of "surplus meaning" is highly problematic and would require much more lengthy discussion to be anything more than a suggestive gesture. I recall that Marx's notion of "surplus value" has a historical component: what is "*more*" than required for social reproduction obviously depends on conditions of identity for what is reproducing itself, and what that will be will change. In the nineteenth century, as Engels points out, producing enough to keep the railways running comes to be part of what is "needed," not a form of surplus or luxury. Similarly, considerations would be expected to hold for "surplus meaning." I am afraid I cannot pursue this any further apart from marking that I think this concept could potentially be important despite its problematic nature.

3. See Hans Blumenberg, *Die Legitimität der Neuzeit* (Suhrkamp, 1966).

4. Hegel, *Werke,* ed. Eva Moldenhauer and Karl Markus Michel (Suhrkamp, 1970), vol. 10, p. 9 (*Enzyklopädie* §377, Z).

5. G. W. F. Hegel, *Differenz des Fichteschen und Schellingschen Systems des Philosophie,* in *Werke,* ed. Eva Moldenhauer and Karl Markus Michel (Suhrkamp, 1970), vol. 2, pp. 20–25.

6. Immanuel Kant, *Kritik der praktischen Vernunft,* ed. Karl Vorländer (Meiner Verlag, 1929), pp. 104–123.

7. From the huge literature on this topic, I mention only Philip Kain, *Schiller, Hegel, and Marx: State, Society, and the Aesthetic Ideal* (McGill–Queen's University Press, 1982).

8. We don't know much about the reforms of Kleisthenes, and what we do know is from later writers, but the later writers, who are the source of most of our information, were themselves Greeks of the fourth century, and they clearly attribute to his reforms the motivation to produce a political structure which will neutralise the effects of significant differences of interests between different regions and tribes. In a city of citizens with as yet undifferentiated interests, no mechanism like this would be necessary. Also remember Plato's account of the psychology of the "democratic man" in the *Republic* (Book VIII).

9. Karl Marx, *Zur Kritik der Hegelschen Rechtsphilosophie,* in *MEW* (Dietz, 1978), vol. 1, pp. 378–380.

10. See T. W. Adorno et al., eds., *Der Positivismusstreit in der deutschen Soziologie* (Luchterhand, 1969).

11. Feuerbach, *Das Wesen des Christentums,* in *Werke in sechs Bänden,* ed. Erich Thies (Suhrkamp, 1975), vol. 5.

12. Sophocles, *Antigone* ll. 360–363.

13. Martin Heidegger, *Sein und Zeit* (Niemeyer, 1963), §§ 46–53.

14. *MEW* vol. 3, p. 33.

15. In his *Zur Genealogie der Moral,* in *Nietzsche Werke: Kritische Studien-Ausgabe,* ed. Giorgio Colli and Mazzino Montinari (de Gruyter, 1967), vol. 5, pp. 245–413; see also "Genealogy as Critique," in *Outside Ethics* (Princeton University Press, 2005), pp. 153–161.

16. St. Paul, after all, in a slightly bizarre passage (*Romans*) seems to claim that the point of the Jewish law was to increase consciousness of sin; one can hold that Christianity generates the sense of sin to which its message of redemption from sin is purportedly the only adequate response.

17. Friedrich Nietzsche, *Kritische Studienausgabe*, ed. Giorgio Colli and Mazzino Montinari (De Gruyter, 1980), vol. 5, p. 266 (*Zur Genealogie der Moral; Erste Abhandlung* § 5).

18. *Antigone*, l. 127f.

19. Landauer, *Revolution* (Rütten and Loening, 1907), p. 13.

20. Landauer, *Revolution*, pp. 37–38.

21. Richard Wagner, *Die Meistersinger von Nürnberg*, act 3 (beginning).

6. Creed, Confession, Manifesto

Epigraphs: Tristan Tzara, *Lampisteries: Sept Manifestes Dada* (Société Nouvelle des Éditions Pauvert, 1979), p. 19; Paul Klee, *Tribüne der Kunst und Zeit. Eine Schriftensammlung. Herausgegeben von Kasimir Edschmid*, Band XIII, *Schöpferische Konfession* (Reiss Verlag, 1920).

1. See Malcolm Bull, *Seeing Things Hidden: Apocalypse, Vision and Totality* (Verso, 2000).

2. What could "create something completely new and different" even mean? Has there ever been any such thing? Isn't in *some* sense anything that exists going to be a reassemblage of previously existing elements? The fact that what is at issue is something *visually* different (and not, so to speak, ontologically different) does not obviously make things easier.

3. Wulf Herzogenrath, ed., *Paul Klee—Lehrer am Bauhaus* (Hauschild Verlag, 2003).

4. *Bauhaus-Manifest*, in *Modell Bauhaus* (Bauhaus-Archiv, 2009), p. 29.

5. Berg, "Lecture on *Wozzeck*" (1929), in *Pro mundo—pro domo*, ed. Bryan Simms (Oxford University Press, 2013).

6. Cf. Heraclitus, Fragment 54. Similarly, in one of his late poems Hölderlin writes "Der König Ödipus hat ein Auge zuviel vielleicht" ["King Oedipus has one eye too many, perhaps"], and Nietzsche's early aesthetic in *Die Geburt der Tragödie* is based on the central claim that too much direct revelation of too much truth would be intolerable for humans.

7. See Plato, *Symposium*.

8. Walter Burkert, *Antike Mysterien: Funktionen und Gehalt* (Beck, 2003).

9. For various reasons early Christians wrote their own history as an exercise is backdating, retrojecting versions of their present as far back into the historical past as they could manage. Thus, once the first Christian creed was created in AD 325, Christians engaged in a search for "more ancient"

versions of the creed, and, when they could find nothing, invented something. Thus, the "Apostle's Creed," supposedly representing a more primitive stage in the development, is first formulated *later* than the Nicene Creed.

10. See Plato's *Socratis apologia.*

11. Heraclitus, Fragments 23–26, in *Fragmente der Vor-Sokratiker,* ed. Hermann Diels / Walter Kranz (Weidmann, 1951).

12. See Lucretius, *de rerum natura.*

13. This is, of course, slightly overdone as an account of freewheeling tolerance of ancient populations in matter of theological speculation because the category of ἀσέβεια ("impiety") did exist and was occasionally invoked for speculative offences. See Aristotle, *Rhetorica* 1399b, reporting something Xenophanes is claimed to have said, and, of course, the case of Socrates. Nevertheless, the basic outlines of the contrast with characteristic henotheist regimes still seem to me important to note.

14. See Thomas Römer, *L'invention de Dieu* (Seuil, 2014); M. Halbertal and A. Margalit, *Idolatry* (Harvard University Press, 1992).

15. Nietzsche speaks of a "maximal god." Nietzsche, *Zur Genealogie der Moral,* in *Friedrich Nietzsche: Kritische Studienausgabe,* ed. Giorgio Colli and Mazzino Montinari (De Gruyter, 1967), vol. 5, p. 330.

16. Reinhart Staats, *Das Glaubensbekenntnis von Nizäa-Konstantinopel: Historische und theologische Grundlagen* (Wissenschaftliche Buchgesellschaft, 1996).

17. In trust the very existence of the agent in whom one places one's trust is not prima facie considered to be up for discussion: of course, Putin *exists,* but should I trust him? Hope is related not so much to the qualities of an individual person whose existence is not in question, but to the possible realisation of a state of affairs that is in doubt.

18. ἀνάστασις νεκρῶν is another formula that recurs repeatedly in early Christian creeds. See Denzinger-Schönmetzer, *Enchridion symbolorum definitionum et declarationum de rebus fidei et morum,* edition XXXVI (Herder, 1965), pp. 31–34.

19. The old term for "creed" is *symbolon,* which means bit of pottery broken irregularly in two so that one can try to fit the two together as a sign of recognition / agreement. This would seem in principle to create a theological difficulty in that the breaks of pottery seem utterly random, but do Christians really want to say that the characteristic elements of their creed are contingent and accidental?

20. M. Weber, *Die protestantischen Sekten und der Geist des Kapitalismus*, in *Gesammelte Schriften zur Religionssoziologie* (Mohr, 1920), vol. 1, pp. 209–213.

21. See Plato's *Socratis apologia.*

22. That the *Manifesto* contains the sketch of arguments for certain theses means that it is not really a manifesto in a pure form, but is edging its way, Marx would say, out of the world of creeds and confessions into that of "science," by which he meant either historically informed philosophy or philosophically informed history.

23. See Martin Heidegger's discussion of ἀλήθεια in various places throughout his work, especially his *Einführung in die Metaphysik* (Niemeyer, 1958), and also the essay "Aletheia," in *Vorträge und Aufsätze, III Teil* (Neske, 1967), pp. 53–78.

24. Tristan Tzara, *Lampisteries: Sept Manifestes Dada* (Société Nouvelle des Éditions Pauvert, 1979), p. 62.

25. "Liberté, liberté: n'étant pas végétarien je ne donne pas de recettes" ["Liberty, liberty: since I am not a vegetarian, I give no recipes"]. Tzara, *Lampisteries,* p. 107. In contrast to, for instance, the highly sectarian surrealists, the Dadaists did not, I think, practice a policy of systematic exclusion of anyone.

26. Available in a more convenient form in A. Schönberg, *Stil und Gedanke* (Fischer, 1976), pp. 189–190.

27. Schönberg does not himself make the point, but one might equally wonder in the light of his remarks about the reliability of the self-observation of religious believers.

28. "Je suis par principe contre les manifestes, comme je suis aussi contre les principes." Tzara, *Lampisteries,* p. 20.

29. Thought initially formulated by Fr. Schlegel in his famous *Athenäums-Fragmente* in the late eighteenth century, developed (in an idiosyncratic way) by Hegel (and also by William James in yet another way), and finally taken up by Adorno.

30. I note that originally, in 1916, this text is *not* called a "manifesto." It acquires that title only upon being reprinted in 1924.

31. Tzara, *Lampisteries,* p. 15.

32. The Brassilow Offensive was perhaps of more significance than may appear to Anglophone readers, given that Tristan Tzara was born Samuel Rosenstock in a small village in the Carpathians, and published his first poems in Bucharest.

33. Friedrich Nietzsche, *Götzendämmerung,* in *Friedrich Nietzsche: Kritische Studienausgabe,* ed. Giorgio Colli and Mazzino Montinari (De Gruyter, 1967), vol. 6, p. 78.

34. The German poet August Stramm, who died on the Eastern Front in September 1915, wrote equally, arguably more extreme, syntax-destroying poems, but, because of the war, they seem not to have been available to the general public until the publication of the celebrated collection *Menschheitsdämmerung,* ed. Kurt Pinthus (E. Rowohlt, 1919).

7. Ivan Is Unwell

1. Herodotus I, pp. 30ff.

2. Guido da Montefeltro appears in Canto 27 of *Inferno,* Buonconte in Canto 5 of *Purgatorio.*

3. There are various English translations. An easily available Russian text with English notes, edited by Michael Beresford, was published by Bristol Classical Press in 2003.

4. T. W. Adorno and Max Horkheimer, *Die Dialektik der Aufklärung* (Fischer, 1969).

8. Metaphysics without Roots

1. Antonin Artaud, *Oeuvres* (Quarto, 2004), p. 1160.

2. Artaud, *Oeuvres,* p. 1639.

3. *Sub rosa* CD (Brussels, 1996).

4. *Althochdeutsche poetische Texte,* ed. Karl Wipf (Reclam, 2002), p. 238f.

5. Wipf, *Althochdeutsche poetische Texte,* p. 236f.

6. "Dies irae," medieval Christian hymn, usually ascribed to Thomas Celano (thirteenth century).

7. *Althochdeutsche poetische Texte,* ed. Karl Wipf (Reclam, 2002), p. 238.

8. See Artaud *Oeuvres,* pp. 1647–1648, for a similar thought.

9. Artaud, *Oeuvres,* p. 1650.

10. Artaud, *Oeuvres,* p. 1652.

11. Nietzsche's *Weh spricht: Vergeh!* (see *Friedrich Nietzsche: Kritische Studienausgabe,* ed. Giorgio Colli and Mazzino Montinari [De Gruyter, 1967], vol. 4, p. 286) is already a dramatic verbalisation of a prelinguistic event.

12. This thesis should not be misunderstood to mean that there is something like a "right of pain to be expressed" (see T. W. Adorno, *Negative Dialektik* [Suhrkamp, 1966], p. 353).

13. Artaud, *Oeuvres*.

14. Artaud, *Oeuvres*.

15. Goethe, *Faust I*, ll. 1338ff.

16. Artaud, *Oeuvres*, p. 1646. Why "crab lice?" Obviously in the first instance because they are bloodsucking parasites. This, however, has a further dimension for Artaud. He thinks the Romans, for example, are a population of crab lice because they "never had another idea in their head apart from securing their own property and treasury by appealing to moral principles" ("L'année où commence cette histoire, l'an 960 et quelques de la dégringolade du Latium: du développement séparé de ce peuple d'esclaves, de marchands, de pirates, incrusté comme des morpions sur la terre des Étrusques; qui n'a jamais fait au point de vue spirituel que de sucer le sang des autres; qui n'a jamais eu d'autre idée que de défendre ses trésors et ses coffres avec des préceptes moraux dessus . . ." Artaud, "Héliogabale ou l'anarchiste couronné," in *Oeuvres*, p. 407).

17. Georg Büchner, "Lenz," in *Lenz; Der Hessische Landbote* (Reclam, 1957), p. 3.

18. Celan, "Der Meridian," in *Werke. Tübinger Ausgabe* (Suhrkamp, 1999), p. 7.

19. Friedrich Hölderlin, "Mnemonsyne" (third version). English translation: Friedrich Hölderlin, *Poems and Fragments*, trans. Michael Hamburger (Anvil, 1994), p. 519.

20. Artaud, *Oeuvres*, p. 1653.

21. Heidegger, *Einführung in die Metaphysik* (Niemeyer, 1957), p. 28.

22. See Guido Schneeberger, *Nachlese zu Heidegger* (Buchdruckeri, 1962), p. 237.

23. Artaud, *Oeuvres*, p. 1641; there are small deviations between the printed text and the version Artaud himself recorded on tape. The printed text reads "le peuple qui mange . . . le délire," but in 1948 Artaud actually recorded "le peuple qui mange. . . . la terre." Those who eat earth need not further roots.

24. Artaud, *Oeuvres*, p. 1672.

Index